D1368108

Who Says Bullies Rule?

Common Sense Tips to Help Your Kids Cope

Catherine DePino

ROWMAN & LITTLEFIELD EDUCATION

A division of
ROWMAN & LITTLEFIELD PUBLISHERS, INC.
Lanham • New York • Toronto • Plymouth, UK

Published by Rowman & Littlefield Education
A division of Rowman & Littlefield Publishers, Inc.
A wholly owned subsidary of The Rowman & Littlefield Publishing Group, Inc.
4501 Forbes Boulevard, Suite 200, Lanham, Maryland 20706
http://www.rowmaneducation.com

Estover Road, Plymouth PL6 7PY, United Kingdom

British Library Cataloguing in Publication Information Available

Library of Congress Cataloging-in-Publication Data
DePino, Catherine.
  Who says bullies rule? : common sense tips to help your kids cope / Catherine DePino.
    p. cm.
  ISBN 978-1-61048-469-5 (cloth : alk. paper) — ISBN 978-1-61048-471-8 (electronic)
  1. Bullying in schools—Prevention. 2. Action research in education. 3. Teachers—
Training of. I. Title.
  LB3013.3.D456 2011
  371.5'8—dc22   2011011152

∞ ™ The paper used in this publication meets the minimum requirements of
American National Standard for Information Sciences—Permanence of Paper
for Printed Library Materials, ANSI/NISO Z39.48-1992.

Printed in the United States of America

To Mary Grace Spinelli, mother, friend, and mentor,
who lived her life with faith and courage.

Requiescat in pace.

We are such stuff as dreams are made on;
and our little life is rounded with a sleep.

Shakespeare–*The Tempest*

Contents

~

Acknowledgments

I'd like to thank Dr. Thomas Koerner, vice president and editorial director, for his helpfulness, kindness, and excellent insights. I'm also grateful to Lindsey Schauer, editorial assistant, for her infinite patience and constant assistance. Thanks also to Della Vaché, assistant managing editor, for her expertise in helping produce this book.

My daughter, Shayna DePino Kudgis, has provided invaluable insights into the world of school counseling in helping bullied children. I'd like to also acknowledge my husband Andrew and daughters, Melissa DePino Cooper and Lauren DePino, for their constant support and love.

~

Introduction

Note to Parents

Can you remember what it felt like to come face-to-face with a teaser, excluder, or a hardcore bully? Do you remember the words, sounds, smells, and sights that surrounded you? If so, you'll want to read this book so that you can help your child lessen and then stop the pain that bullying causes.

Who Says Bullies Rule? offers specific tips you can give your child to prevent bullying before it begins. It also gives tips for stopping bullying before it gets too hard to handle. With your help, your children will know when they can deal with a bullying episode themselves and when to turn to an adult for help.

What can you tell your children about their own appearance so that they won't become easy targets for bullies? Some children aren't aware that how they dress and act can attract a bully's attention. Learn how the way children walk, talk, or move makes them easy prey for harassment.

Also, *Who Says Bullies Rule?* underscores the importance of working together with the school to help your children ward off bullies. You'll need to know how to use the channels in your school system to get the best results possible for your child.

Additionally, this book also gives advice about dealing with the different types of bullying that your children will most likely encounter.

Perhaps the most important feature of this book is that it addresses the significance of having your children pay attention to their common sense to anticipate and deal with bullies' actions.

Even the youngest children can use their common sense to evaluate teasing to know if it is a silly joke or something more serious. They can develop the ability to sense which areas in the school and in the neighborhood to avoid, thus preventing someone from harming them physically or emotionally. Moreover, they will use their common sense to know when to react and when to ignore bullying.

I'll talk about the importance of constant communication with your child on a daily basis so that you know exactly where your child stands when it comes to his or her peer group.

Once you help your children deal with bullying, they will enjoy the peace and freedom that is everyone's birthright. When your children learn to use common sense coupled with bully prevention techniques, they will not be afraid to go to school, to take the school bus, or to have lunch in the school cafeteria.

No child should ever have to tolerate physical or mental abuse at the hands of a bully. You are the first line of defense against bullying. This book will show you what to do to help keep your child safe, but moreover, to empower your child to deal with bullying.

Introduction

Note to Educators

If you're an educator reading this book, you know the importance of working with children and parents in preventing and stopping bullying. Very often you are the first one to learn that a bully is harassing a child. You know what a vital role you play in preventing and stopping this damaging behavior by educating children and parents.

Perhaps the most important thing you can do is to keep parents informed if you suspect their child's experiencing bullying. That's not an easy order with everything else you're called to do during the school day, but it could mean the difference between life and death in some cases. We've seen the havoc bullying can cause with the rash of depression and suicides in children of all ages in recent years.

If you are a school administrator, you may want to consider giving a copy of this book to PTA members to encourage them to work together with the schools to prevent and stop bullying at all grade levels.

It is only when we are willing to work together as a team and to keep one another informed about bullying that we will gain momentum in our goal of putting an end to the bullying cycle that is claiming our kids' peace of mind, and, in all too many cases, their lives.

Note

To avoid awkwardness in language usage, I alternate the pronouns *he* and *she* throughout this text.

CHAPTER ONE

Keep Your Child a Step ahead of Bullying

Beware: Bullies Can Strike Anywhere

As a teacher, I've witnessed many types of bullying: name-calling, teasing, hitting, ignoring, cyber bullying—you name it. I've seen bullying in the classroom, the lunchroom, the gym, the bathroom, the school yard, the school bus, in the neighborhood, and on Facebook. Some kids have confided that their own brothers, sisters, and cousins shun them, call them unspeakable names, or beat them up in their own homes.

In one inner-city school, kids who earned good grades avoided the lunchroom for fear their classmates would attack them, so they took their lunch to an empty classroom and ate alone. Others chose to eat lunch with a teacher who'd befriended them. They did this on the sly, fearful of risking a bully's revenge, which could range from taunts about being the teacher's pet to a fierce beating.

Most bullying victims hesitate to seek help because they're afraid the bullies will retaliate and subject them to worse tortures. They believe they have no choice but to live in dread of the bully's next attack. They don't want to take school or public transportation for fear of getting beaten up; they hold off using the bathroom because bullies hang out there; and they avoid the school yard, where bullies often lie in wait.

Many bullied kids offer excuses for not wanting to go to school: they have a stomach virus, the teacher doesn't like them, or school bores them. A few end up with school phobia and experience psychological pain when entering a school building. Some cut classes and end up in the discipline office.

Parents often don't know what's going on until the assistant principal tells them to come to school to reinstate their child after suspension. Even then, some kids will never tell the real reason they won't go to school.

Kids facing bullying often take one of two paths: they fight back, which often backfires, or they set themselves off from their families and friends, eating alone, and locking themselves in their rooms for hours, where they watch TV, play video games, or surf the Internet in search of virtual friends. Sadly, sometimes they find themselves meeting up with virtual bullies.

What can you do to help protect your children from bullies without making them dependent on you to solve their problems? You can arm them with techniques to ward off bullies, while at the same time teaching them self-reliance and creativity in finding answers to any bullying problems they encounter. Once you set them on the right path, they'll know what to do. But you'll need to be there in case they need backup when bullies badger them.

Start Bully-Proofing Early

If you teach your children about dealing with bullies from a very young age *before* they start school, you will give them a head start in knowing what to do when a bully strikes.

Begin your bully education program before your children experience bullying, so that they will recognize bullying when they see it and find effective ways to deal with it. Because you've taken the time to be proactive, your children will have more options in knowing what to say or do to stop the bully.

They will be prepared and know how to respond to bullies because you and your child have discussed techniques in advance, role-played, and talked about what types of responses work best in different situations.

Even at an early age, some instances of bullying will jump out at your children, so they can't help but know something isn't right. Here's an example:

Stacey, a kindergarten student, positioned herself next to her friends on the rug at story time. Maria sat next to her.

Stacey looked at her and whispered something to a classmate.

Stacey pointed to the spot next to the teacher. "Move over there. There's no room here. You can't sit with us."

"Why not?" Maria asked.

Stacey wrinkled her nose. "Your clothes are ugly, and I can't understand you when you talk."

Why was Stacey treating her like this? Although Stacey and her friends stuck together and didn't play with Maria at recess, Stacey had never said anything like this to her before.

She wondered if she should tell the teacher or try talking to Stacey first. She knew she had to do something, but what?

If Maria and her mother had discussed different types of bullying such as exclusion (kidspeak: not allowing someone to sit with her or join an activity), she might have known some different ways to respond.

In this case, since the bullying had just started and hadn't yet escalated, Maria's mother may want to talk to her about first trying to deal with it herself. Maybe Maria could try telling Stacey that she didn't like what she said.

On the other hand, if Stacey laughs or ignores her, Maria may want to talk to the teacher privately, or her mother may want to discuss the problem with the teacher, especially since Maria is in kindergarten.

If the teacher intervenes and the situation worsens, the teacher may want to contact Stacey's mother and meet with the school counselor to discuss the bullying.

Your children should know from an early age when to try to handle the problem on their own or when to ask an adult (parent/counselor/school administrator) for help; namely, when the bullying becomes constant or severe.

Kids also need to know that they can depend on an adult to handle the situation in a way that will not open them up to retaliation by the bully. Emphasize to your children that they can feel free to tell you anything and that you will help them deal with their problems in a way that will make them feel safe and protected.

Share Your Experiences

As your child learns how to recognize and learn helpful responses to different types of bullying, you, your child's siblings, grandparents, and extended family may want to discuss bullying situations you've encountered in the past and challenges you've faced in solving them.

However, before telling your story, try listening without judgment to your child's concerns about his own problems. Let your child know that you've truly listened by making a comment once he's told you what happened. For example, you could say, "That must have been really hard for you." Then you can tell your story to show that he will eventually find a solution just as you did.

Seeing that you or someone you know has experienced bullying will help your child put a bullying incident in perspective and know that it will eventually come to an end.

I believe that you, the parent, can be your child's greatest ally in preventing bullying and in keeping bullies away. But you need to have the right tools so that you can be an advocate for your child, helping to solve the problem once a bully strikes and speaking up to school and law-enforcement authorities if you need to.

Above all, teach your children to use common sense to prevent bullying and to stop it from getting worse. How can you best teach common sense? Some parents think you either have it or you don't. They see it as something you're born with, like a talent for playing the ukulele or making dunk shots.

However, many people believe that children can learn common sense by example and practice. Chapter 2 addresses helping your child use common sense, a major tool in the fight against bullying.

KEY POINTS: Chapter 1

- Arm your children with techniques to deter bullies. Teach them independence and creativity in dealing with bullies.
- Always be available in case your children need help with bullying problems.
- Discuss how to deal with bullies before your children start school.
- Involve the entire family (parents, siblings, grandparents, etc.,) in the bully prevention process.
- First, listen. Then talk about your own experiences with bullying: what happened, what you did, the challenges you faced, and the outcome.

~

CHAPTER TWO

Encourage Your Child to Use Common Sense to Outsmart a Bully

Model Common Sense

Encourage your children to use common sense to help keep bullies away and to give them a good sense of knowing what to do when bullies attack. Let them see you using common sense in situations you deal with every day.

Modeling common sense in everyday choices and decisions you make will go a long way in teaching them to use it in their own lives.

Imagine you're watching a home-shopping channel and think the clothes advertised would give you a stylish new look. You crave that red ruffled dress, but do you need it? Will you give in to temptation and order it in every color?

Or, what about this scene? You see a new gizmo for your car that would make hands-free talking on the phone much easier. It's not in the stores and it costs a bundle. But how will you do without it?

You can model common sense by talking to your child about how the advertised item appeals to you and how much you'd like to buy it. But you can also bring into the conversation some things you'll need to consider before spending your money. In this way, your child will see that you're using good judgment in deciding what to do, which brings us to this scene:

Your child sees you thinking about your dilemma: to buy or not to buy.

"Why don't you just send for it if you like it that much?" she asks.

You might then ask her to give the negatives of buying the item. She's already seen you mulling over the positives. She might say that it looks like it costs too much or that it's not a good idea to buy things without first seeing them.

5

By having these conversations and asking her to give input on making decisions, your child will learn about using common sense in all areas of life.

Help Your Child Use Common Sense and Logic to Make Decisions

Besides modeling and discussing your own experiences using common sense, how else can you inspire your children to use it in their everyday activities? In the course of your children's day, many occasions will arise that pose an opportunity for using common sense to help gain insight into different problems—and not only those related to bullying.

Have your children ask questions about different situations in their lives and come up with smart answers that use both gut feelings and logic. After all, isn't that what common sense is all about: using our best instincts along with logical reasoning to make decisions? Isn't that what we all do when trying to make good decisions in all areas of our lives?

Give Practice Using Common Sense in Bullying Situations

If you have a preschool child facing bullying, offer a variety of options and ask him to choose the best one. For example, if a neighbor child keeps grabbing your preschool child's toys and monopolizing them, what's the best way for your child to react? One choice would be to walk away and play with something else, another would be to tell the child to stop, and a third would be to tell a parent.

Have your child consider all the circumstances surrounding each bullying event to help determine which would be the best course of action in each case. If your child feels that walking away from the situation for a short time would be a good solution, he may want to try that first.

On the other hand, if your child has known the other child for a long time and doesn't think that telling her to stop would work, she may want to ask you to intervene.

Instead of saying, "Cara won't give me back my game," she might want to diffuse the situation with a little humor, saying something to you like, "Dad, I think we need a referee. Can you help?"

Common sense will go a long way in helping your child deal with bullying issues. If the neighbor child has a temper and your child thinks he may retaliate physically or verbally, your child will want to tell you in confidence. On the other hand, if it's an isolated incident, your child may simply say something like, "If you keep doing this, we won't be able to play anymore."

As a rule, bullies act more complex and sophisticated with elementary and middle-school students than they do with younger children. Your child may find them more difficult to figure out. Say your elementary child is getting dirty looks and snubs from a member of the popular crowd. Is it best for her to ignore the bully, talk to the child one-on-one about how the behavior hurts, or tell the teacher?

It will help your child to consider how other kids in the class have dealt with this child in the past. What has worked or not worked? If the bully has a track record of getting other kids to ignore one child, or if no one can talk to her and get her to listen, it's time for your child to talk privately with the teacher.

Here's another example of using common sense to deal with a bully, involving a fourth grader. A few kids in Dion's fourth-grade class tease him because he wears bifocals and carries a few extra pounds on his short frame. Dion didn't tell his mother Kia about the teasing because he felt embarrassed. However, one day when she picked him up from school, she heard a classmate calling him "fatty" and "four eyes."

When they got home, Kia poured Dion a glass of lemonade. "I know what you're going through," she said.

Dion pushed the lemonade aside. "How could you know?" he asked. "You never wore big glasses, and you weren't fat like me."

Kia smiled. "Yes, but I stuttered, and the kids at school called me 'Porky Pig.' Believe me, I understand."

Dion took a sip of the lemonade. "So what did you do?"

"I tried ignoring the kids, but they wouldn't stop. But one day, my friends Jackie and Nicole let those kids know they didn't think treating me that way was fair."

"I can't picture kids in my class doing that," Dion said. "How did they say it?"

"Actually, Jackie came right out with it. She said, 'How would you feel if someone made fun of you because of something you couldn't help?'"

Was this his mother talking? From what his aunts and grandmother had told him, he'd always thought of her as one of the popular kids when she was growing up, certainly not like him.

"What did the kids who were bugging you do then?" he asked.

"At first, the kids who teased me laughed and called my friends 'teachers' pets,' but they didn't tease me quite as much after that."

"Any teasing is a pain," Dion said. "Did they ever stop?"

"Eventually. When some other kids joined my friends in speaking out against the bullies, they gradually stopped bugging me."

"Why was that?" Dion asked.

"All it took was a group of kids who wanted to help me to bring an end to it," Kia said. "In those days we called them 'friends helping friends.' Today we call them 'bystanders.'"

"I could use some bystanders now," Dion said.

Kia put out a plate of oatmeal cookies even though they hadn't eaten dinner yet. "Believe me, son, I know what you're going through because I've been there."

Dion grabbed a cookie. "Do you think it would help if I stayed around friends more?"

"Good idea," she said, "especially when you're at recess where the bullying seems worse, from what you tell me. The other day you mentioned that you might want to try talking to the boy who seems to be the leader of the kids bullying you. Do you think it's safe, or do you think you should see your counselor right away?"

With these questions in mind, Dion, with his mom's help, built a plan to stop the bullies. Kia wrote down ideas as she and Dion brainstormed a solution. After they discussed their ideas, they crossed out those they didn't think would work and highlighted in yellow the ones they thought would help. Since Dion was the one experiencing the bullying, he made the final decision about which techniques to try.

Every day when Dion got home from school, he and Kia discussed how the plan was working for him. When Dion said that something wasn't helping, they discussed what other ideas he might try.

Here are the things Dion decided to consider in his plan to stop the teasing: thinking about how they've acted before, do I think I can talk to these kids and tell them how I feel about what they're saying, or would it be better to wait a while longer and see what happens?

Often, using common sense to figure out what makes a bully act the way he does will give your child helpful clues about how to react.

Also, encouraging your child to use common sense in figuring out a plan for stopping the bully will, in many cases, give your child insight into developing a reliable plan to stop the bully.

Dion considered a few more questions in his plan to stop the bullies:

If they don't stop bothering me, which adults (besides my parents) should I talk to? Which ones would be the most likely to help me? If that person doesn't help stop the problem, whom should I talk to next?

How can my friends help me stop the bullying?

What are some things I can do to buoy myself up while someone is bullying me?

In the end, Dion decided that he couldn't ignore the bullying any longer and that he had to do something. He also felt that talking to the kids who bothered him wouldn't help because his attempts to reason with them in the past had only resulted in more mistreatment by them.

After talking over his plan with his mom, Dion decided to talk to his counselor without his mother present. He also asked his friends to stay near him in the school yard and in the lunchroom. His friends also marshaled other kids' support. Whenever these kids were around, the bullying did not seem as frequent or severe.

Of course, it often takes more than a peer support network to stop a bully from bothering your child. But if done diligently and consistently, bystanders, especially in a group, backing your child, works like a charm. No kid, not even a bully, can battle a group of kids banding together to protect another child.

Dion also decided to spend more time playing baseball with his friends and to stop moping around the house and playing video games by himself. Thinking about the bullying only made things worse.

He found that actively doing something every time he felt helpless at the hands of the bullies relieved much of his sadness, anger, and anxiety. With his mother's and the counselor's help, Dion set his plan in motion. Within a few short weeks, the bullies backed off, and he began to enjoy his life as a happy fourth grader.

Dion decided that if the bullies started bothering him again, he'd continue trying all his ideas and think of some new ones. He made up his mind to stick to his goal of breaking away from the bullies.

If you present your children with opportunities to use common sense in daily interactions with friends and family members, when they meet up with bullies, they'll feel more at ease in using these techniques to find solutions to both simple and complex bullying problems.

Maybe someone is spreading nasty tales about your middle-school child on the Internet. Should she confront the bully and ask why she is doing this, or should she tell you immediately? If your child's common sense sprang into action, she would know that Internet bullying is hard to handle without help.

In this type of bullying, the perpetrator could say even worse things because the bullying is more anonymous. For this reason, your child should immediately talk to you about what's happening so that you could contact the local authorities to stop the harassment.

However, many kids wait to seek help, not because they're lacking in common sense, but because the subject never came up before in conversations with their parents. That's why it helps to discuss commonsense solutions to bullying problems with your child before things get out of hand.

Using common sense will help your children gain the ability to tell the difference between the teasing that goes on between friends and outright harassment. It will help them know which kids to choose as friends and which ones to avoid. It will also keep them away from places where bullies gather and help them know which places to avoid and when to avoid them.

Consider these questions that children like yours grapple with every day: What should I do if my friend ignores me? What if the kids on the bus keep calling me names? Who would help me if someone stole my jacket from my locker? What do I do if someone tells lies about me on the Internet? Suppose someone threatens to beat me up because he doesn't like the way I look? What if someone makes fun of the way I talk?

When problems like this surface, your children can rely on their common sense to get them through the rough spots. If you give them practice in using their common sense before issues like this come up, they will be better prepared to deal with them.

How can using common sense help your child deal with appearance-based put-downs? What if your children want to express their individuality to such an extent that it makes them butt heads with their classmates? Suppose they can't help the way they look and kids bully them?

What about kids who attract their peers' negative attention because they try too hard? Maybe your child is a victim of random bullying, that is, bullying that occurs for no apparent reason. Chapter 3 addresses appearance-based bullying and shows how you can help your child deal with it by using common sense.

KEY POINTS: Chapter 2

- Encourage your children to use common sense to help keep bullies away and to give them a sense of knowing what to do when bullies attack.
- Model common sense in making everyday decisions.
- Ask your children for input when modeling common sense.
- Encourage your children to use both common sense and logic in daily decisions.
- Have your children consider circumstances surrounding each bullying episode to help determine which would be the best course of action to take.
- Ask your children key questions to help them come up with effective bullying solutions.

~

CHAPTER THREE

Bully-Proof Your Child against Appearance-Based Put-Downs

Why Should Your Child Care What Others Think?

Did you ever notice how some kids are open targets for bullies? That's because in the school and school yard, whether it be kindergarten or high school, appearance counts. That's not saying your child needs to be a clone of the other kids: dressing, moving, and talking as they do, losing his individuality to the pack.

However, your child needs to know that if she's radically different from her peers in the ways she looks, talks, and uses body language, her classmates will probably notice. And sometimes they'll respond in unkind or dangerous ways.

Is this blaming the victim? Some people might think so, but why should your child wave a red flag in front of bullies if she knows that certain things she does will cause them to bother her? It's simply common sense to know what sets off bullies and to have your child avoid looking and acting so drastically different from her peers that they'll take it as an invitation to harass her.

Certainly, your child can keep his individuality in the midst of conforming classmates, but it's not smart to flaunt it to the extent that he stands out in a way that would invite classmates' teasing, heckling, hitting, or worse.

Simple things like personal hygiene, tooth brushing, and hair washing can make a huge difference in how peers perceive your child. Also, whether your child stands straight or slouches, and whether she sports a confident or downbeat expression work in tandem with appearance to cause other kids to see her in a positive light or as potential bully bait.

Many kids ask why they should care what other people think. What's wrong with expressing themselves with their own unique clothing and hairstyles? Why can't they be who they are without fearing that others will intimidate them because they are different in one way or another?

Like it or not, people judge us and our kids on our appearance and on how we project ourselves to those around us. If we don't smear on deodorant, gargle with mouthwash, forget to dig out the crud from our fingernails, and wash our hair until it squeaks, someone will definitely notice.

Most kids don't know how to tell some of their classmates that those nasty kids in the lunchroom (school yard, bathroom, hallways) are making their lives miserable because they don't bathe or change their socks often enough. Instead, they go along with the crowd and turn into bullies themselves, or they stand by, watch it happen, and do nothing to stop it.

In the adult world, appearance can mean the difference between a job and the unemployment line, between having friends or being lonely, and between being relaxed and confident or wondering what's wrong and how you can fix it. In a child's world, appearance can make the difference between having friends or living in isolation, fear, and anxiety.

By the way, this is the only place in this book you'll see some preventive things parents can do to forestall bullying by advising kids about how to dress and act. The bottom line is that it's never appropriate to ridicule anyone for any reason.

However, looking at it from a commonsense standpoint, it helps to know what kinds of actions on our kids' parts may contribute to bullying. It's helpful because we're living in a world where bullies will use any excuse to tease or torment their victims, and we don't want to give them a reason to act out their fantasies, not if we can help it. And in some cases, such as the ones listed, we can.

What Can You Do to Help Stop Appearance-Based Put-Downs?

There are some commonsense things you can do to help prevent your child from facing appearance-based bullying. Check him out before he leaves the house. If he looks a lot different (in an unusual or far-out way) from the other kids in his class, it's time to talk.

You may not be up on the latest clothing or hairstyles, but you'll know if he stands out in a way that might make the other kids pick on him.

Some kids draw attention to themselves by their unusual appearance or by ignoring personal hygiene. (Bad smells, such as body odor and bad breath seem to elicit the most teasing.) Some kids become prey for bullies by appearing overly shy or nervous. Others alienate their classmates by trying too hard to make friends. You know your child better than anyone else, and you know what things could cause other kids to harass or exclude him.

As we know from our own childhoods, kids could razz us to death for no reason other than that we looked or acted differently from the crowd. While we want to be sure that our kids honor who they are as individuals, it helps to remind them not to look, dress, or act so differently that bullies will be tempted to abuse them.

Why "No Kid of Mine Leaves the House Looking like a Freak" Won't Work

By now, you're probably wondering how you can convince your child not to go out of the house looking like Count Dracula or Frankenstein's Bride. It's hard enough getting kids to wear clean underwear and brush their teeth. You know from experience that screaming, punishing, and nagging won't work. So what can you do, short of locking them in their rooms, when they look like the lead in a vampire flick or pierce every visible body orifice?

The sad fact is that if you haven't established who's in charge early on, it's hard to start later, and *later*, these days, means the middle grades. We're talking fourth, fifth, and sixth. But be assured that no matter how old your child is there are things you can do to help change the status quo.

It's Never Too Late

If your child is a victim of appearance-based bullying, there are some things you and she can try. Offer to take her shopping for new clothes with practical guidelines she can live with in mind: "stylish, but not outrageous" being the operating words.

Suppose you both have different ideas about what *stylish* means? Push for a compromise, something along the lines of this for a girl: "That top you're wearing looks like it goes with bikini bottoms. But if you layer it, and use it as a camisole under this shirt, you've got the look."

For a boy, you might point out that maybe jeans a size or two smaller would look better than ones that drop to his navel, exposing the less flattering parts of his anatomy. Kids in a school where I used to teach loved baggy pants and called them "vict pants." They thought that imitating prisoners' (convicts') styles made them look cool to their friends.

Another thing you can do is give your child the once-over before she leaves for school. If she's wearing something that doesn't jibe with your dress code or the school's, tell her that she needs to choose another outfit. And make it stick.

Talk to your child about how it's okay for him to be an individual in the way he dresses—within reasonable limits. If his clothing and hairstyles become outrageous, he may open himself up to bullying.

Read the story of two kids who wanted to be different but got more than they bargained for in the bullying department.

I Just Want to Be Me

Sean and his friend Keith, eighth graders in a city middle school, styled their straggly, dyed, platinum hair in ponytails, like members of the British parliament in times past, and wore only tight, dark-colored clothes. Since grade school, they felt they had nothing in common with the other kids. They weren't interested in school activities, like sports and dances, and viewed their classmates as boring and clueless.

Despite protestations from their parents and complaints from their teachers, the boys refused to modify their hair and clothing styles. The school's dress code had banned obscene tee shirts and revealing styles but posted nothing about hairstyles and clothing colors.

Their teachers got frustrated with their classmates harassing them and the disruption it caused in class, and they ended up reporting the boys to the vice principal. Their classrooms had become a sideshow, which more than once escalated to profanity and threats from the bullies and loud laughter from classmates. Custodians complained about obscene graffiti in the bathroom describing the boys' bizarre appearance.

Their parents tried reasoning with the boys, then moved on to punishment such as grounding, to get the boys to modify their dress, but they wouldn't hear it. Eventually, the parents gave in and stopped preaching to their sons about their unusual look, thinking it was a phase that they'd grow out of.

Kids taunted the boys from day one, calling them "weirdos," "freaks," and "faggots." One day in the school yard, things came to a head. A pack of jocks on the JV football team picked a fight with them and beat them up because "they looked like freaks and gave the school a bad name."

Sean and Keith fought back physically and escaped with a few cuts and scrapes, but their attackers outnumbered them and started harassing them everywhere they went: in the classroom, the bathroom, the cafeteria, and on the school bus.

No one made a move to help the pair because even the kids who didn't openly bully them thought they deserved it. Fearing retaliation, the small group of kids who considered themselves apart from the crowd didn't dare seek help.

After the attack, the assistant principal suspended the ringleaders, but she also warned Sean and Keith that she would suspend them for insubordination if they refused to modify their hair and clothing styles. She knew she was on shaky ground legally, telling the boys how they should dress and style their hair, but things had gotten out of control, and she didn't know what else to do.

The school counselor backed up the assistant principal, suggesting to the boys and their parents that if they dressed more conventionally the bullies would be more likely to ease up on them.

But Keith and Sean weren't buying it even though they knew that failing to cooperate with the administrator would throw them into "in-school suspension," a dismal basement room presided over by a teacher who bore a strong resemblance to Quasimodo and assigned endless pages of boring busywork.

"We just want to be who we are," Keith told his counselor.

"We don't expect the other kids to look like us," Sean added.

"Throw us in the jug (their name for in-school suspension). At least nobody will bother us there," Keith said, holding his ground.

"Go home and think about it," the assistant principal said. "If you don't make some changes within a couple of days, we'll have no choice but to suspend you."

If All Else Fails, Use Common Sense

Knowing from past history that their kids wouldn't budge, Sean and Keith's parents brainstormed in search of a solution. Both sets of parents admitted that they were at an impasse with their sons and wanted to try a new approach. But what could possibly work?

"This may be a long shot," Keith's mother Barb said, "but the guys were talking about this big concert that's coming to town in a couple of weeks."

"What does that have to do with solving the problem?" Sean's dad, Andrew, asked.

Barb wondered if she was taking the right route, but her common sense told her it was worth a try. "The concert's only here for one appearance. The boys want to go, but they said they wouldn't be able to come up with enough money."

Her husband, Matt, gave her a look. "Are you saying we should pay for the tickets? Sounds like a bribe to me."

"Every time they put on those grotesque outfits are we supposed to give them a reward to look like normal kids?" Andrew asked. "A bribe would teach them to be more manipulative. We're looking for a change, and mollycoddling them will only make things worse."

"Hear me out," Barb said. "We could use the tickets as an incentive for the boys to start cooperating."

Her husband nodded. "You're figuring that will make them come around to our way of thinking?"

"Maybe," Barb said, "and maybe not. But I say we give it a try."

"I guess we could try it," Matt said. "Nothing else seems to work."

"I'm in," Sean's mother, Sue, said.

Andrew shook his head. "I'm not so sure."

"Looks like three of us want to try it." Barb said.

Andrew hesitated. "It looks like I'm overruled. And we have tried everything else."

That afternoon the parents told the boys about their incentive. Just as Barb thought, Sean and Keith agreed to compromise on their appearance. They also agreed to keep the lines of communication open (within reason) between themselves, their parents, and the counselor.

The boys showed up for school the next day in jeans and rock band tee shirts that helped them express their individuality but yet blended in with the other students' styles.

They hated giving up their unique hairstyles, but decided to compromise by letting a stylist clip a couple of inches off their unkempt locks. They also started letting their natural hair colors grow back in.

In the meantime, with the counselor's help, they learned not to respond to the teasing. Instead, they walked away whenever someone whistled or called them "weirdo" or "gay." When that didn't work, they used assertive body language and told the hecklers in calm but insistent voices to stop bothering them. With the counselor, they practiced using assertive responses on each other.

"Lay off," Keith said when Sean, taking the part of a bully, called him a "faggot."

"I'm not taking that," Sean said, in a strong voice when Keith, acting out the bully's role, called him a "one-man freak show."

All the while, per the assistant principal's request, the boys kept their parents and the counselor informed of the bullies' responses. If the counselor thought that their assertiveness wasn't working and that the bullies were coming back at them full force, he'd alert school security without delay.

The parents kept in close touch with the school to make sure the teachers and administrators were backing them by enforcing the district's anti-bullying policy. If they weren't satisfied, they'd sit down with the counselor, teacher, and vice principal to air their grievances and say they needed more support from them to make the plan stick.

"Ask for the help you need and don't be shy" was their motto. The parents hoped that with the support of home, school, and the school security force, the plan might work. At the same time, they were realistic enough to know that even the best plans sometimes backfire with bullies.

Taken aback by their new image and different response tactics, the boys' classmates gradually stopped teasing them. Within the next couple of months, a chess team member they knew through their interest in the sport asked them to sit at his lunch table. Gradually, Sean and Keith built a small network of friends and joined the school chess team, something they would never have agreed to before. With the counselor's and assistant principal's continuing help, the boys' parents were able to regain better rapport with their sons and to restore some measure of harmony in their homes. This is not to say that family life reached perfection in the two households.

The boys still argued with their parents about what they thought were unfair rules about early school-night curfews, smoking, and excessive video-game playing. As their sons began to compromise, their parents gradually gave them additional privileges, which made the boys cooperate more.

In Keith and Sean's case, an incentive worked as the catalyst to move them to compromise with their parents, but if that doesn't work with your child, keep trying until you find something that does. Use your creativity and knowledge of what has moved your child to cooperate in the past to see what will work in your case to motivate your child to turn things around.

If you think about what has worked before, you'll probably say that hollering, nagging, and put-downs always proved useless. Instead, try reasoning, compromise, and negotiation. You'll have a better chance of getting your point across that way.

Sometimes, as in the case of Keith and Sean, small things work better than elaborately planned strategies. Get together with the parents of your child's friends who are also experiencing bullying. You and the other parents can brainstorm about the way you've approached bullying problems in the past. If your ideas worked for your child, try them again. If you weren't satisfied with the results, come up with something new. It may be the breakthrough you need to put an end to the bullying.

What if nothing works? You've tried everything and your child continues a behavior pattern that works against her? Then start looking for professional help for your child. Ask the school counselor or your doctor for a referral. If you're not satisfied with the progress your child is making with one therapist, find someone else. But don't wait too long.

What If Your Child Looks or Acts Differently Through No Fault of Her Own?

Maybe your child has a physical or mental disability that opens him up to harassment from other kids. Most schools teach students about respecting differences, but some kids continue to harass these kids no matter what anyone says.

Maybe the child bothering your child has a mean streak or likes to hold power over someone who finds self-defense difficult. The reason doesn't matter. How your child decides to approach the problem does.

If your child experiences bullying because of something she didn't cause, you can help her use all of the techniques in this book. Using common sense often means taking a simple, straightforward approach to a big problem. Sometimes a simple explanation by a child with special needs can deter a potential bully. If doing this doesn't help, your child needs to find an adult at school she trusts and tell that person what's happening.

Look at the next example to see a case where a budding bullying problem was stopped cold due to a classmate's simple explanation of her disability.

Amanda, a third grader, wears conspicuous hearing aids in both ears.

Beth, a classmate, laughed at her in the lunchroom. "I've seen old ladies in my great-grandmom's retirement home wearing hearing aids like yours. They look weird on you."

Amanda smiled and said, "You're right. My aids are kind of clunky, but they help me hear everything you're saying, so I'd appreciate it if you'd say only nice things."

Beth, surprised by her classmate's candor and easy spirit, said, "Sorry. I'll try to remember that."

In this case, Amanda's forthright explanation helped educate a potential bully and stopped future problems before they had a chance to escalate. However, as with all other bullying encounters, you'll want to advise your child to seek help from an adult if she needs it.

What if Your Child Tries Too Hard?

At the opposite end of the spectrum from Keith and Sean, the boys who got hassled because they wanted to be different, bullies sometimes pursue kids who appear too perfect and conforming.

Take a look at an example of a suburban middle-school counselor's report to the assistant principal. It shows what sometimes happens when a child tries too hard to win approval from her peers. Maple View Middle is a zero-tolerance school, and bullying episodes are carefully documented and monitored.

From: Dr. Thaddeus Bently, School Counselor

To: Ms. Lauren Simpson, Assistant Principal and Dean of Discipline, Maple View Middle School

Subject: Report on Irina Pavlova, Grade 6

I am enclosing the summary and outcome you requested, related to bullying episodes experienced by Irina Pavlova, a sixth grader in the honors program.

This mature looking, well-spoken young woman wears the latest fashions, styles her hair long and straight like the popular girls, and excels in softball. She told me she never thought she'd become a bullying victim. However, for the past three months, the girls in her class have made her life miserable by taunting her in a variety of ways.

Irina attempts to cover up her lack of self-esteem by bragging to her classmates about her accomplishments in her schoolwork and on the hockey field. Her teachers have reported that she further alienates her peers by staying after school to help them mark papers and decorate bulletin boards.

Some girls in her class began shunning Irina and calling her *kiss up* behind her back. Marissa, one of the popular girls, spread rumors about Irina, saying that she shoplifted and stole money from a classmate.

Marissa and a couple of her classmates launched an Internet campaign against Irina, advising her classmates to have nothing to do with her because of the alleged (but totally unsubstantiated) shoplifting allegations. They posted messages on Myspace and Facebook and started a texting campaign to turn her class against her.

When Irina's mother Natalie asked why she never heard from any of her friends, she said they were all snobs and she'd rather have no friends.

As Natalie's concern about Irina's unpopularity grew, she began monitoring her daughter's phone conversations and reading her journal. Natalie told me that when Irina found out, she stopped confiding in her.

Eventually, shut off from the other girls, Irina began talking to her mother again. Happy to give advice, Natalie told Irina that if she wanted to have friends she had to be a friend and take the initiative. But it seemed that the harder Irina tried, the less the girls wanted to be around her.

In hopes of winning her classmates' affection, and with her mother's prodding, Irina invited all the girls in the class to her birthday extravaganza, dinner at a Japanese steak house, a sleepover with movies, hot fudge sundaes, and goody bags filled with gift certificates to their favorite stores at the mall.

Things came to a head when only three girls out of fifteen agreed to attend. Irina canceled the party and spent the day picking at pizza and birthday cake in her back yard with only her parents and her pet Schnauzer in attendance. She spent the night crying in her room.

Meanwhile, classmates continued to call Irina names and exclude her from their activities. During one of her weekly visits to my office, I told Natalie that she needed to step back and give her daughter some say in solving the problem. She agreed, and this marked the beginning of the end of her daughter's problems.

Using her common sense, Irina decided that she would stop trying too hard to gain her classmates' acceptance. She made plans to spend more time with her one close friend doing things she enjoyed, like going to dance class and riding bikes in the park.

Eventually, when some of the other girls saw that Irina had changed her approach, a few of them started talking to her. She asked two of these girls to join her and her friend on a bike ride, and they accepted. She never became close to the girls who had spread rumors about her, but they stopped bothering her and she learned to coexist with them.

I will continue to observe the situation with Irina and will stay in touch with Natalie with weekly phone calls. If the situation deteriorates, I will alert you and security promptly so that you can take action. For now, things remain stable.

The counselor noted in a subsequent conversation with the assistant principal that once Natalie gave Irina the freedom to devise a plan she thought would work for her, her situation improved.

Sometimes stepping aside and giving your children a voice in solving their problems will empower them to begin looking for commonsense solutions to bullying, solutions that will work for them because they had a say in developing them.

Sometimes we look for complex answers to bullying problems and neglect to see how commonsense solutions can help kids come out on top. Trusting our children to think of simple yet effective resolutions to big problems often works better than parents and school staff mapping out a complicated plan for them. At the same time, they need to know that the adults they depend on are standing by to help whenever they're needed.

Sometimes Bullies Choose Their Victims Randomly

Bullies don't always pick their victims based on appearance, how they move or talk, or because they have a disability or are simply different from them. Sometimes there's no reason at all, or a feeble one at best. Maybe a bully has chosen your child as a victim because he happened to be in the wrong place at the wrong time or because his parents grounded him and he felt like taking his anger out on somebody.

When this kind of bully strikes, there's usually no warning. Any small act on an innocent victim's part can set the bully in motion. However, if your child thinks about it, she may have seen this type of bully strike before. Maybe the student in question cursed out another student in the lunch line because she took too long to decide between fries or macaroni and cheese. Or maybe she shoved a classmate on the playground because she thought a girl in the in-crowd stole her best friend.

You can tell your child to deal with the bully who strikes for no apparent reason the same way he deals with a bully who thinks he has a reason to pick on your child—although we know there's never any legitimate reason for bullying.

Because this type of bully's attack is swift and sudden, and often severe, your child will have to act quickly and may not have time to use speech, body language, or humor to deflect the attack. In this case, common sense would prompt your child to tell the closest adult, meaning the teacher, lunchroom monitor, hall guard, or administrator.

Encourage your child to tell you if someone's bothering him, no matter what the circumstances. It's common sense to keep parents and school staff informed with any type of bullying. Let your children know that they can depend on you and other caring adults to help them.

In addition to becoming aware of the reasons (or lack of obvious ones) that bullies attack, you'll want to discuss with your child how to deal with different kinds of bullies; namely, those who ignore, exclude, tease, insult, or intimidate, bully their siblings, or cyber bully. See chapters 4 and 5 to learn how these different types of bullies can bother your child and what you can do about it.

KEY POINTS: Chapter 3

- Keep an eye on your children's personal hygiene and clothing styles. Be sure they look presentable before leaving the house.
- Know what causes appearance-based put-downs generally and for your child specifically.
- Use diplomacy and tact in getting your children to make a presentable appearance.
- Use incentives to help your children revamp their images.
- If incentives don't work, try other positive strategies such as reasoning, compromise, or negotiation. Avoid negative consequences such as yelling, nagging, and put-downs.
- If you don't feel your efforts are helping, seek professional help. If one therapist doesn't work out, find another.
- If your children try too hard to gain popularity and end up being bullied, support them, but prompt them to think of ways to solve their problems.
- Tell your children to seek an adult's help quickly in the event of random and sudden bullying.
- Stress to your children that if they're dealing with any type of bullying, they can depend on you and other caring adults to assist them.

~

CHAPTER FOUR

Help Your Child Deal with Bullies Who Ignore, Exclude, Insult, or Intimidate

What Can You Do about a Bully Who Ignores Your Child?

Do you remember what it felt like to be ignored, or not to be included when your classmates played at recess? Maybe you weren't invited to a party that most of your friends attended, or maybe a child you considered a friend talked behind your back.

Being ignored or excluded can make your child feel lonely and left out. It can also prompt her to ask: "Why don't they like me?" "Why didn't they invite me?" "What's wrong with me?"

By the same token, it's helpful for kids who experience ignoring or exclusion to face the fact that in life not everyone is going to be your friend or want to be with you. And the stark truth is that you can't force other children to be friends with your child. Although kids should learn to deal with rejection in the form of being excluded from school activities and parties, they should also be aware of when these actions cross the line into unkind behavior and bullying (often in the form of teasing and name-calling).

To get an idea of the effects of excluding and ignoring on children, let's eavesdrop on Leah, a fifth grader whose classmates shun her and talk behind her back:

Leah is about to take Punim, her pet Yorkie, for a walk. She locks the leash in her collar and heads toward the door. Shayna, her mom, looks up from her computer.

Shayna: Why don't you give Punim a treat and take her out later so we can talk?

Leah invites the dog to settle in her lap and gives her a treat.

Shayna: How was school today? Are things any better?

Leah: Those girls I told you about are still ignoring me. But since the counselor talked to them, they've stopped saying mean things.

Shayna: I'd say that's some progress. And you have your own friends, so you can do things with them. If the other girls don't want to talk to you, does it matter that much?

Leah: I guess not—as long as they aren't calling me names and making fun of me.

Shayna: So why don't you invite a couple of your friends to go to the movies this weekend? I'll drive, and you can see if Sarah's mom can pick up.

Leah: That sounds like fun. I'll call Sarah after I take Punim out.

Shayna: I know it hurts when some kids don't want to be your friend, but we can't always control what people do, right?

Leah: I guess I'm lucky to have a couple of good friends like Sarah and Jen. Thanks, Mom. I'm glad you're always here to listen.

Shayna: If anything changes, or if you just need to talk, let me know. Okay?

Leah throws her mom a kiss and races out the door with Punim.

It's clear that Shayna is keeping on top of Leah's bullying problem and that Leah feels free to talk to her. And if the problem resurfaces, they'll discuss what to do. Leah will make the final decision about any bullying issues, using her common sense and taking her mother's good advice into consideration.

What If Someone Excludes Your Child?

Bullying involving excluding other children happens more often with girls although boys are certainly not immune to it. When children bully other kids by causing damage to their social standing or relationships with a group, it goes under the umbrella of "relational aggression."

Children from all age groups experience ignoring and exclusion. There's no one way to deal with it, but parents can keep in close contact with the school, a ripe venue for forming cliques, talking behind other kids' backs, or blocking peers from participating in recess games.

When any of these exclusionary events happen, there's nothing much a parent can do after the fact. That's why it makes sense to push for a school anti-bullying curriculum (preferably one that reaches across the curriculum and is reinforced in every subject) that heightens children's sensitivities to excluding other kids from events.

Work with your school principal and the parents' group at school to ensure that the school addresses how excluding children affects their sense of self-worth and offers solutions kids and parents can live with.

For example, it would help to have a school policy that doesn't allow children to hand out invitations to a birthday party in school. They could call the children at home or send invitations in the mail, so that the children who aren't invited wouldn't feel excluded. Also, if a child invites most of the class, it would be courteous to invite the few remaining students to spare hurt feelings.

Imagine this scene: Rosa, a second grader new to her school, is one of three girls in her class not invited to Dana's birthday party on Saturday.

Alex, her custodial parent, finds her crying in her room when he comes home from work.

Alex: What's the matter, Rosa?

Rosa: Dana didn't invite me to her party. I thought we were friends. We play together every day at recess.

Alex: I'm so sorry, honey. I wish there was something I could do. Maybe I could ask the counselor to see if she has any ideas.

Rosa: Daddy, please don't do that. If she finds out, she really won't want me to be her friend.

Alex: Okay. It's up to you. Sometimes things like this happen for no reason. Maybe she could invite only so many people. But that doesn't help you feel better. Sometimes things like this happen, and it hurts, but it doesn't mean she doesn't like you.

Rosa: I still feel sad, Daddy.

Alex: I can see that you do. I'll tell you what: Why don't you invite some of your friends from the neighborhood and the girls who weren't invited to Dana's party to come over on Saturday? We'll play some games in the backyard and have a barbecue.

Rosa: Thanks, Daddy. That would be fun.

In this case, Alex gave Rosa the option of his calling the counselor to get her insights into the situation. However, he respected her wishes, and he came up with an alternative plan that involved inviting her friends to her home for a get together. In this case, his common sense told him that it wasn't necessary to involve the counselor at this point.

Although not being invited to the party hurt her deeply, she would have the chance to enjoy the company of other children, and the sting wouldn't hurt quite as badly. Her father also validated Rosa's hurt feelings by listening to what she said and acting on it.

Here's the story of Binh, a fourth grader, who's rarely asked by the other kids to play ball at recess. His parents, Danh and Kim, notice that he's been withdrawn at home lately.

Danh: Why do you not want to go to school? Every morning we have to struggle to get you to the bus on time.

Binh: I don't like school.

Kim: Your teacher says you're doing well in your tests. What is it that you don't like?

Binh: The kids don't want to play with me. They say I look different and I don't talk like they do.

Danh: We are all different. That's what makes us interesting. It would be pretty boring if we all looked and acted the same, wouldn't it?

Binh: I guess so. But sometimes I wish I were more like them. Maybe then I would have more friends.

Kim: I understand, son. But you're fine the way you are. Now we'll have to think about how to make things better at school.

Danh: Maybe we could talk to your teacher and see what she thinks.

Binh: Then she might tell those kids, and they'll really hate me.

Danh: I don't think they'll hate you once they get to know you. If they do, it's their loss.

Kim: We'll ask the teacher not to say anything. But we'll all put our heads together. We want you to like school. I know we can find an answer.

In this story, Binh's parents listened and confirmed his feelings of sadness that kids were excluding him. The next week, they made an appointment with Binh's teacher. They agreed that her plan to have the children discuss their family customs and bring in pictures of their relatives would help the class gain an appreciation for other cultures. Binh planned to bring in pictures of his cousins who lived in Vietnam and to talk about what school is like for them, their foods, and what they enjoy doing on the weekends.

With any type of bullying problem, open communication between you and your child helps ensure a positive outcome. Think about dispensing advice to your child in short doses. It also helps to listen, to refrain from talking too much, and to feel comfortable with silence while your child formulates thoughts and questions.

Sticks and Stones Will Break My Bones and Names *Can* Hurt Me

Of the many types of bullies your child might meet, teasers are the most common. Before working out a strategy to deal with teasers, your child will want to think about the nature of the teasing. Is the teaser being nasty or merely joking in a silly manner without the intention of hurting someone?

Very often, your child will be able to use her instincts to zero in on the nature and severity of the teasing. Her common sense will tell her whether it's a serious tearing down of her personality or appearance or horseplay that doesn't have a cruel intent.

When your child feels that the teasing hits hard or constantly happens, it's time to talk to an adult. If you create a climate where he feels safe telling you anything, he'll feel free to talk about things that happen during the school day.

If your child feels upset about the teasing or if it goes on for a while, she'll know when she needs to tell. She'll know because she'll feel that something is not right—that she needs relief from the hurt that she's feeling.

If the teasing happens at school, it's wise for your child to talk to a teacher or counselor and to relate exactly what's happening. Of course, your child may back away from telling because he fears that the bully will treat him worse.

However, if your child knows how to ask for help with the assurance that the school worker will not let on that she said anything, she will feel safer in reporting cruel or recurrent teasing.

If your child is hurling his own silly jibes at the teaser, then it's a mutual thing, but that doesn't mean it's not treading in dangerous territory. Sometimes even harmless jokes can have an edge that borders on insult or cruelty. That's why it's best to caution your child to stay away from teasing, name-calling, and insults, and not to engage in them as sport because horseplay, even among friends, can turn destructive in a matter of seconds.

Show Zero Tolerance for Insults

Sometimes kids uses terms like *faggot*, *gay*, *ho* (short for whore), and "your mama" insults to tease their friends and enemies. Although early elementary children use these words because they've heard older kids using them, they're more likely to use words such as *doofus*, *kiss up*, or *cry baby* to taunt their peers. You'll want to talk to your children about avoiding this type of teasing as it can rapidly mushroom into verbal and physical abuse.

Here's a case in point: Antoine and his friend James, fifth graders, are tossing a ball around at recess. Antoine starts playing with James to see how far he can go before his friend strikes back.

"Your mama has false teeth and looks so fat she bursts out of her clothes."

James stops throwing the ball. "Oh, yeah? Your mama eats dead whale intestines and throws them up all over your daddy's new car."

Antoine gets up in James' face. "Your mama has such bad breath you have to put clothes pins on your nose."

James grabs Antoine by his collar and is about to punch him when Mr. Williams, the teacher on recess duty, sees what they're doing and takes them both to the office for fighting.

"He started it," James says. "Why am I in trouble?"

"You're both in trouble," Mr. Williams says. "And I thought you two were best friends."

"We are," Antoine says. "We were only playing."

"Friends are kind to one another. They don't say mean things or touch one another in anger." Mr. Williams says.

"Okay, we're cool," James says.

"We won't do it again," Antoine echoes.

"I hope not," Mr. Williams says. "Just to be sure, I'm going to call your parents. You'll have some explaining to do when you get home."

"For real?" James asks. "Can't you cut us a break, Mr. Williams?"

"If I did that, you wouldn't think twice before you did it again," the teacher says. "Case closed."

In this incident, the teacher was proactive in that he didn't ignore the boys' teasing one another when they went over the line. He set limits and gave consequences. He went a step further by contacting their parents to help ensure it wouldn't happen again.

Whether or not your school is a "no tolerance school," the reality is that sometimes the school staff is too busy to watch every child all the time. Bullying events can fly under their radar because their attention is somewhere else. Also, school personnel are often tempted to overlook fracases among kids because they think they should try to solve their own problems. That's why it helps for you and other parents to monitor the school's awareness of bullying problems and its efforts to rectify them.

Use Caution in Dealing with Intimidators

Watch out for intimidators because the way they torment kids is usually more heavy-handed than is the way of kids who tease or insult. They're often more aggressive and believe that they can get kids to do anything they want (hand over money, homework, jackets, cell phones, for example) without anyone challenging them. They're also not above using physical force to get their way or to reinforce whom they think owns the power.

They often show adults the same defiant attitude they foist on kids. Sometimes they use a stealthy and secretive approach, believing they're immune to getting caught. Other times, they're in-your-face, out in the open with no concern about consequences for hurting your child. Either way, it's hard to win with an intimidator.

How can you best counsel your child to deal with this type of bully? If the bullying presents as psychological intimidation rather than physical intimidation, your child may want to try speaking firmly to the perpetrator.

However, your child first has to access her common sense in determining whether she can even attempt to talk to this bully who wants her new iPod, essay answers, or boyfriend, for example. Some intimidators don't want anything your child owns. Their main goal is to harass someone who is different from them.

But be forewarned: It's crucial not to waste words when dealing with a bully who gets physical. Your child needs to get help immediately.

In this case, your child should try to make a fast getaway, scream as if in a flame-filled room to draw a crowd, or get help at once from a teacher, administrator, or school security officer.

In line with this, your child should know where the school security office is and should be able to identify the school security or police officer. That way, if he ever faces bullying, he'll know where to go immediately for help, especially if a teacher, counselor, or administrator is unavailable.

Let's look at a case of psychological and physical intimidation in which a student had to decide whether to deal with the bully herself or to seek help.

Ava, an eighth grader, thought she heard her classmate Sofia talking about going out with Ava's boyfriend Luís. Actually, Sofia was talking about dating Luís' friend Robert, but Ava wouldn't believe her. Ava corners Sofia in the school cafeteria.

Ava: Stay away from my boyfriend or I'll get my girls to beat you up.

Sofia: I'm not interested in Luís. He's not my type. I was talking about Robert to those girls. I told them Robert asked me to go to the football game.

Ava: I don't believe that. You're a liar. I saw how you looked at him at the dance. I've got my eye on you, girl. So watch it.

At this point, seeing Ava's body language (eyes narrowed, arms folded) and hearing her angry, threatening voice, Sofia's common sense told her that trying to reason with Ava would prove futile. Using clues picked up by the senses (in this case, sight and hearing) will enhance your child's ability to zero in on a bully's intentions and to act accordingly.

Sofia discussed the situation with her mother, Celia, who agreed that it would be best for both of them to go to the principal instead of Sofia going alone since Sofia knew that last month Ava and her friends had threatened another girl at the subway stop for not giving Ava her homework to copy. Ava was, without a doubt, someone to watch out for.

Sophia and Celia felt that it would be smart to have her mother along for support since Ava posed a distinct physical danger to her. The next day they went to the principal, who referred the case to the school police officer.

Because of Ava's previous episode of intimidating another student at the subway stop and this more recent case involving Sofia, the principal recommended that she be monitored closely and that if her actions persisted, she would push for transfer to a disciplinary school.

Now we'll view a case of psychological intimidation in which a student decides to handle things differently because of the circumstances surrounding the intimidation.

Nathan and Sanjay are in the same seventh grade social studies class. For a long time Nathan has been bothering Sanjay to write his research paper. Sanjay earns straight A's, and Nathan does not like to do schoolwork. Why should he when he can convince Sanjay to write his papers for him? After all, it's worked before.

Nathan: Sanjay, buddy, I need a favor.

Sanjay: No more favors. You need to do your own work.

Nathan: Don't mess with me. You know I'm a boxer, and I can hit you where it hurts.

Sanjay: I don't want to hear that.

Nathan: You're saying you won't help me?

Sanjay: I'm saying I won't write your paper. You'll have to find a way yourself.

Nathan: What kind of friend is that?

Sanjay: I work at the tutoring center. You can come there after school and I, or someone there, will help you get started.

Nathan sighs and walks away.

In this case, Sanjay knew from thinking about his past encounters with Nathan asking him for his work that he talked big but didn't carry out his threats. When Sanjay countered with "I don't want to hear that," Nathan backed down.

Nathan looked like an intimidator but Sanjay believed he was all talk, or Sanjay wouldn't have responded the way he did. His common sense would have told him to report the incident.

In the end, Nathan never took Sanjay up on his offer to help and ended up failing the class. Even though Sanjay's instincts told him that Nathan was more talk than action, he decided that if Nathan threatened him again physically he would talk to his counselor. He also informed his parents about this and past encounters with Nathan. He wasn't about to take any chances.

Generate Creative Ideas about Bullying Problems

One thing you can do to help with any type of bullying is to take the time to generate creative ideas with your children about how to deal with the type of bullying they're facing. Find a time when you're both relaxed and feel like putting your heads together to think of a variety of ideas about how to deal with the problem.

Record the solutions you both come up with, and then highlight the ones in yellow marker that your child thinks would help for his individual situation. Ask him to try ones he thinks will help remedy the problem.

Let's look in on Cara, a nine-year-old, and Justine, her mother, discussing Cara's recent encounter with Lena, a girl in her class who excludes her from playing with her and her friends at recess. They're considering whether it's best for Cara to deal with the problem herself or to inform a school authority immediately.

Justine: You said that Lena was calling you names and wouldn't let you play tag. What was she saying?

Cara: She calls me "blubber butt" and "ugly." The thing is I don't want to play with her because she's mean, but I like some of her friends.

Justine: How do the other girls treat you when they're with Lena?

Cara: They want me to play. A couple of them said so. But they're afraid Lena will make fun of them if they let me. Lena's always in charge. So they ignore me too.

Justine: What do you think would help?

Cara: She thinks for a few minutes, and Justine keeps quiet, giving her a chance to answer. I guess I could stay away from her and play with Tess, my friend who doesn't get along with Lena either.

Justine: That sounds like it might work. But what will you do if Lena keeps calling you names and she and the other girls keep leaving you out?

Cara: without hesitating. I know I don't want to talk to her about it. I've tried that. She never listens and makes fun of me more.

Justine: How would you feel about talking to your counselor about it, and how long do you think you should wait if you decide to?

Cara: I think I'll give it a couple more days of not staying around her, which is pretty hard because she always seems to be where I am. I'll hang out with Tess. If Lena keeps bothering me, I'll talk to my counselor. Maybe he'll have some good ideas. He helped Tess when some girls in our class were mean to her.

Justine: I can see you've been thinking about some ideas that might work. Let me know how it goes tomorrow. Okay?

Cara: Okay, I guess, Mom. And thanks.

For the next couple of days Cara did her best to stay clear of Lena and spent her time sitting on the school steps playing handheld video games with her friend Tess.

On the fourth day, Lena strode up to where they were sitting and asked Cara why she was hiding from her. Cara firmly replied that she wanted her to leave her alone, but Lena refused to leave, saying nobody but Tess liked her because she was "fat and disgusting."

Later that day, Cara knew it was time to see her counselor. After he heard her story, Mr. Jamison stopped by Cara's classroom and escorted Lena to his office, where they had a long talk about her behavior toward Cara. Mr. Jamison, with a classroom aide's help, monitored her dealings with Cara in class and at recess.

The counselor also met with her parents and continued to discuss Cara's feelings about the bullying with her and her mother. In a short time, Lena stopped bothering Cara. She knew that her parents, who also worked to eliminate her bullying behavior, and the counselor weren't going away until she changed her ways. In time, the other girls in her crowd stood up for Cara, insisting that she be included in their recess games.

The talks between Cara and her mother helped arrest a bullying problem before it veered out of control. Cara used her common sense in coming up with a workable solution. She knew when it was time to talk to her counselor, and she acted on it, thus saving herself a protracted bout of aggravation.

When your child has direct input into what is happening to him, he will feel better prepared to deal with any future bullying problems. Also, this will give him a chance to use common sense in coming up with solutions.

Each time he works out a solution that brings him release from a bully's clutches, he will grow in confidence. Working with you to help generate creative ideas to address the problem will help him achieve that goal. And if he doesn't, he will have the satisfaction of trying again with a different approach if the bullying recurs.

In chapter 5, we'll look at two types of bullying that present a great challenge for many children and their parents: sibling bullying and cyber bullying.

Bullying by a brother or sister is one of the most difficult types to control as the perpetrators live in the same home, and the victims can't avoid them because they taunt them around the clock.

Parents are often the last to know about the severity and intensity of the bullying, as the bullied sibling often fears strong reprisals.

Many experts believe that cyber bullying tops all other types of harassment in the harm it inflicts on children. Much of it is secretive and anonymous. It's often hard to tell whom the bully is.

More often than not, cyber bullies show little or no remorse for the pain they inflict on their prey. They can't see how the victim is affected because they can't see their facial expressions or reactions, and even if they could, they probably wouldn't care.

KEY POINTS: Chapter 4

- Keep in close contact with the school, a ripe venue for forming cliques, talking behind other kids' backs, or blocking peers from participating in recess games. Know what's going on.
- Push for a school anti-bullying curriculum that heightens children's sensitivities to leaving kids out.
- Practice open communication with your children to ensure a positive outcome.
- Dispense advice to your children in short doses.
- Listen, refrain from talking too much, and feel comfortable with the silence while your children formulate thoughts and questions.
- Inform your children that it's time to talk to an adult if teasing hits hard or occurs constantly.
- Advise your children to refrain from teasing, name-calling, and insults, and encourage them not to engage in them as sport.
- Tell your children to avoid wasting words when dealing with a bully who gets physical and to get help immediately.
- Generate creative ideas with your children about how to deal with the types of bullying they're facing.

CHAPTER FIVE

~

Help Your Child Deal with Sibling Bullying and Cyber Bullying

Suppose the Bully Lives in Your Own Home?

Let's face it. Your children are going to fight. Sometimes they'll test your limits and leave you wondering what you did to make them act this way. But don't blame yourself. All kids argue although some argue more often and more loudly than do others. Sometimes you wonder if they'll ever grow out of it.

When should you start to worry about your children's fighting? You'll know you have to take strong action when your children go beyond the limits of what you think is normal fighting among brothers and sisters.

As with all types of bullying, when the words your kids use cut into the core of the other sibling, or when the fighting turns physical with hitting or punching, you'll have to act immediately. But ideally, you'll do something before that point, before sibling rivalry turns into bullying. You'll also know that you have to do something if the fighting never stops and you find yourself totally frazzled by the day's end.

Kids can fight over the most trivial things: who gets the most pieces of pizza, who gets to sit in the front seat of the car, or who gets to watch a favorite TV show. But it stops being trivial when one child attacks a sibling's personality by constantly insulting or degrading her.

What can you do about sibling bullying? Primarily, you can use your best instincts about what makes your own kids act the way they do. For instance, if one tends to wage sneak attacks when nobody's looking, keep them in your range of vision whenever you can.

Also, if one child acts more contentious when he's tired, be sure he gets a nap if he's rubbing his eyes and acting out. Another thing you can do is keep a record of which child's turn it is to choose a TV show, a favorite dinner, or a game.

It always helps to recognize your children for something they do uniquely well and to compliment them specifically rather than generally. One child aces tests, and the other shows leadership skills by working with the student government or being captain of a sports team. Showing favoritism, sometimes without realizing it, fosters a breeding ground for bad blood between brothers and sisters.

Along with this, don't take sides in arguments although it may sometimes be advisable when the identity of the culprit is blatantly obvious and you want to bring the fighting to a quick resolution. If both children are bickering in a way that's not abusive, you may want to give the same consequence, such as no video games or TV, for whatever time you think is fair, to both children.

The main thing you'll want to work toward is a relatively peaceful sibling relationship, and one that is always free of physical and mental abuse.

State strongly and often your policy about bullying. Create a simple statement that reflects how you expect your children to act toward one another. Repeat the statement whenever bullying occurs and after you impose consequences for the actions.

Eventually, your kids will get the idea that you aren't going to tolerate them treating each other badly. Here are a couple of things you can say, or make up what you believe will work with your children: "I don't want to see you act this way anymore. No more foul language and no more hitting—ever again" or "I expect you to treat your (brother/sister) with kindness and respect. Expect consequences every time you break this rule."

State your expectations and the consequences for not meeting them regarding sibling disagreements. Be brief and concise. The more you talk, the less your kids will listen.

Remain consistent in enforcing what you tell your children you will do if they disregard your rules about getting along. If you don't give consequences, even one time, your children won't think you mean what you say and will continue to disregard your rules for living civilly in your home.

It's also beneficial to praise your children when you catch them getting along. Name the behavior you want to reinforce. Say something like, "You're both working on that puzzle together so nicely. That's how we like to see you getting along"; "Not one argument today! Doesn't that feel better than hitting or screaming at one another?"; or "I'm glad to see you helping your brother with his homework. He's really learning how to solve those math problems because of you."

It's as equally important to give praise as it is to mete out consequences. Positive usually trumps negative approaches when working with your children toward a goal: in this case, fewer fights and a complete stop to ugly, destructive bouts.

Give compliments when you see your children getting along, but don't get carried away. Too many compliments can be worse than none at all. If you find that the fights become severe or that you're unable to stop them, you'll want to contact a therapist. Your school counselor may also have some good suggestions.

Move Quickly When Bullying Gets Out of Control

Here's an example of bullying behavior between a brother Chad, who's five and in kindergarten, and his sister Brooke, age eight, in second grade. So far, the children have engaged in standard sibling fighting, including name-calling, and bickering. However, today for the first time, Brooke forcefully hits Chad over the head with a hardcover book.

Chad runs into the kitchen crying loudly to Jay, his Dad.

Chad: Brooke hit me hard. *He shows Jay a lump on his head.* Jay examines the lump and hugs Chad.

Jay: angry, but trying to remain calm. Brooke, come in here.

Brooke: I didn't mean it, Daddy. He kept calling me "stupid" and he scribbled on the picture I was drawing.

Jay: No excuses. That's not a reason to hurt him. *He shows Brooke the lump on Chad's head.*

Brooke: starting to cry. I'm sorry, Daddy. I won't do it again.

Jay: It's not me you have to apologize to. You need to tell Chad. What you did was serious. You could have really hurt your brother.

Brooke: moving toward Chad. I'm sorry for hurting you. I was angry, and I wasn't thinking. I didn't mean to do it.

Chad, still crying, clings to his father.

Jay: Not thinking is never an excuse. You always need to think about what you do. In this house we don't hit or hurt people.

Brooke: Okay, Daddy.

Jay: Now I want you to go up to your room. No TV for tonight. And think about one nice thing you can do for your brother tomorrow, one kind action to show you're truly sorry.

Brooke goes to her room, leaving Jay to put an ice bag on Chad's head.

The next day, after school, Brooke invites Chad to share her prized art supplies and apologizes to him once again.

In this instance, Jay acted quickly in reprimanding Brooke. He told her there's never any reason to use your hands to hurt. He listed the expectations for how family members should treat one another. He then gave her what he thought were appropriate consequences for treating her brother the way she did. Jay believed that any kind of hitting or emotional abuse must be addressed immediately.

Here's a case of sibling bullying, this time between two sisters.

Jade, age twelve, and Tanya, age thirteen, can't be in the same room lately without fighting physically and calling each other abusive names. Shawna, their mother, has tried everything—lecturing, yelling, and grounding—but the girls persist in using foul language and hitting each other, sometimes causing injuries like scratches and bruises.

The latest episode ended in Tanya giving Jade a black eye. Shawna treated it herself as she was fearful that if she showed up at the ER, medical personnel, thinking she'd abused her daughter, would notify Family Services.

The next day, despite Shawna's best efforts, Jade's eye looked worse. Shawna took her to the family doctor. Of course, the doctor questioned Shawna about the injury, thinking it may be child abuse or school bullying. Shawna told her about how the girls fought. She advised family counseling and recommended a therapist who specialized in sibling problems.

After a few weeks of therapy, the girls learned to settle their problems in a peaceful way. They will probably never get along the way Shawna had hoped, but at least it was a start.

Read on to find out why cyber bullying is one of the most virulent forms of harassment a child can face.

Be Aware of Your Child's Cyber Connections

Cyber bullying is serious business. Many children face depression, and more than a few kids have committed suicide because of it. Bullies are becoming increasing savvy in using texting, IM's, e-mails, the Internet's social networking sites, cell phones, and Webcams as means to harass kids and to sometimes ruin their lives.

Very often, children may not be aware that they're being recorded and their words and photos widely disseminated so that peers can watch their personal business blatantly exposed in a text, e-mail, or Webcam video. Their most private thoughts and actions unfold for all their peers to view and ridicule.

Cyber bullying often involves spreading rumors and talking about a child's personal life to complete strangers. Once someone spreads malicious talk about a child on the Internet, it is impossible to counteract the damage. The child is held up in shame for all the world to see, and no one can undo it.

For this reason, it's a good idea to monitor your child's Internet usage and to explain to your child why you have to do this. You'll need to be aware of all passwords and accounts. Does this mean you have to oversee all of your child's Internet communications? Besides being impractical for you, it would give your child reason to think you don't trust her to use her best judgment. But you'll want to explain that the reason you're keeping an eye on her Internet comings and goings is because you want her to be safe. To drive this point home, share articles and newscasts with your child about kids who have faced irreparable damage at the hands of cyber bullies.

One major thing you can do to know if your child is experiencing cyber bullying is to use your instincts to tap into his moods before and after he uses the Internet or cell phone. Does he look unduly agitated or sad? Does he spend a lot of time alone in his room?

Of course, these are all signs of normal childhood and teenage moodiness, but if they intensify or linger for a prolonged period of time, especially in conjunction with your child using a cell phone or computer, it's time to connect the dots.

There are many unscrupulous people (adults and children alike) who take advantage of children on the Internet by trying to ruin their reputations or attempting to snare them into meeting up with someone who could harm them physically and emotionally.

It's wise to continue setting up an environment where your child will feel free to tell you everything when it concerns bullying of any kind, especially Internet bullying where the stakes are high.

Whispering Down the Cyber Lane

Here's a scene involving Kelly, a sixth-grade girl whose classmates are spreading rumors about her on the Internet. It started as a texting campaign by Mia, a popular girl on the cheerleading squad, who disliked Kelly because she thought she was stealing her best friend.

Soon after, Mia plastered Kelly's picture hugging a boy in their class with the word *skank* scrawled across it on social networking sites frequented by their classmates. The picture showed Kelly's friend, whom she'd never been romantically involved with, innocently hugging her at a birthday party.

Kelly's mother Julie, with whom she's always had a close relationship, has noticed Kelly acting withdrawn and uncommunicative. The only time she spends time with her parents and sister is at dinner. Then, she retreats to her room.

Kelly's parents keep the computer in the family room so that their children's use of it is monitored at least as far as time spent on it. They also ask her to leave her cell phone (equipped with the Internet) downstairs before bedtime, as they know that she and her sister like to use it late into the night. Another thing they insist upon is that they know all the passwords their girls use.

After Kelly completes her homework at the dining room table, Julie heads for her room.

Julie: Kelly, let's talk.

Kelly: What about, Mom?

Julie: I know something's bothering you. You can tell me.

Kelly: starts to cry. I can't.

Julie: You never had trouble before.

Kelly: I'm so upset. I don't know how to say it or what to do.

Julie waits until Kelly is ready to talk. She knows that if she probes or pushes, Kelly won't tell her what's wrong. That's always been her pattern ever since she was a young child. And Julie finds that respecting that helps Kelly open up.

Kelly: Mom, Mia is talking about me to kids at school, and she's posting stuff that isn't true all over the Internet.

Julie: What kind of stuff?

Kelly: That I do things with boys, things I'm not into.

Julie: You need to show me.

Kelly: Are you sure you want to see it?

Julie: Yes. Whatever it is, we can do something to stop it.

Kelly shows her mother the picture with the cutting word.

Julie: That is really mean of her to do that. We'll contact your counselor tomorrow and see whether we should talk to the school officer. Also, I know that our state has laws against cyber bullying, so we'll ask about that.

Kelly: Meanwhile, I'll stay away from her at school. I think I'll stay away from the computer for a while too.

Julie: Good thinking. And remember that anyone who knows you does not believe it's true. We'll work together with the school to put a stop to whatever goes on there. And if the bullying continues outside of school, we'll need to contact the police.

Kelly: Thanks, Mom. I still feel terrible, but knowing we're doing something to stop it makes me feel a little better.

Julie: I'm glad we talked.

Kelly: So am I.

Because Julie had made a habit of talking freely with her daughter, solving this problem was easier. The next day, Julie contacted the counselor who invited the school police officer into the conference. The officer confirmed that there were laws against cyber bullying in their state. Kelly contacted the local authorities, and they dealt with Mia's actions in accordance with these laws.

Record All Events

If you learn that your child is a victim of cyber bullying, it would help if you and your child keep a dated record of the events should you need to contact the police. Be sure to include names (if you know them), websites, and what was said about your child. Also, print out from the computer what was said about your child.

If the bullying involves peers at school, inform the counselor and principal so that they, along with school security, can intervene at their level. Everyone has a stake in beating cyber bullying, and the home and school need to be in sync to gain positive and rapid results.

Don't wait until the problem flies out of control and it's too hard to do anything about it. Strive to get your child to open up about everything, especially bullying. If you don't know what's going on, you can't help.

As soon as you know that your child is dealing with cyber bullying, contact the local police. Be aware of the cyber bullying laws in your state in case you need to take additional steps to help your child become free of the bullies.

Ensure that your Internet connection is safe so that bullies can't easily access your child's personal data. Similarly, your child should not give too much information about her personal identity on Facebook, Myspace, and similar sites, as this will make her easy prey for a cyber bully. Warn her not to talk to people that she doesn't know on the Internet.

One of the most significant decisions your child will have to make in dealing with bullying is when and how to talk to the bully. He'll want to use his common sense and best instincts to help him decide these questions: Is it ever wise to talk back to a bully? If so, what are the best things to say, and what should you never say? How can your child figure out what makes a bully think the way he does? Will making a joke provoke or help a bullying incident? What kinds of things can your child do to appear stronger and more confident in front of a bully?

Chapter 6 will give your child ideas about how to respond or not respond to a bully in a variety of situations.

KEY POINTS: Chapter 5

- Showing favoritism, sometimes without realizing it, fosters a breeding ground for bad blood between brothers and sisters.
- State strongly and often your policy about sibling bullying.
- Be brief. The more you talk, the less your kids will listen.
- Be consistent in enforcing what you tell your children about what you will do if they disregard your rules.
- Monitor your children's Internet usage, explaining why you need to do this.
- Share articles and newscasts with your children about kids who have faced irreparable damage at the hands of cyber bullies.
- Keep a dated record of the events of a cyber bullying episode, should you need to contact the authorities.
- Be aware of the cyber bullying laws in your state in case you need to take additional steps to help your children become free of bullies.

CHAPTER SIX

~

How to Talk So a Bully Will Listen

Does It Help to Ignore the Bully?

Sometimes with silly, low-level teasing that all kids dish out, particularly with friends, it may help your child to turn a deaf ear to the bully and to not acknowledge it. If the teaser doesn't have an audience, he may figure it's not worth his while to tease your child.

However, most big-time bullies are persistent and won't be deterred by someone not paying attention to their pushy bids for attention. Talk to your child about using her instincts to tell whether the teasing is serious enough to warrant some kind of response.

He'll know that it's time to say something to the bully if he feels demeaned by the bully's words or actions. He'll be prompted to take action in the form of an assertive response, or, if the situation warrants, to take action in the form of informing you and school personnel.

If You Want to Give a Bully a Message, Make It Loud and Clear

Make no mistake about it: bullies know what they're doing when they make the decision to harass your child. They're not misunderstood victims dealt a bad break by their parents, their schools, or society. And so what if they were? Your children never deserve to be abused by them, and they need to stand up to bullies if they believe it will help, *believe* being the operating word.

They will know when to talk to a bully because their common sense will tell them if it would be a wise or foolish decision. They should never attempt to talk to a bully if it would place them in physical or psychological jeopardy.

If they decide to respond to a bully's insults, tell them to use as few words as possible and to speak clearly and firmly. Most people tune out too much talking or explaining and often take wordiness as a sign of weakness. Short responses of one or few words such as "Stop that," or "Don't say that," will get the message across more effectively.

Here's a look at a bully who hurls racial slurs against a classmate, and how the young man reacts with words.

Len, a ten-year-old Native American, attends Front Street Elementary. He's made a couple of good friends and likes his teacher, Ms. Patel, but Cory, a boy in his class, has started using racial slurs against Len every chance he gets.

Cory stops at Len's desk on the way to his seat in math class. Len looks over his homework, hoping that Cory won't say anything. He's tried hard to avoid a showdown, but he feels that now is the time to say something if Cory bothers him.

Ms. Patel is helping a student in the back of the room.

Cory: *laughing.* When are you going back to the reservation with all the other savages?

Len: *looking up at Cory.* Don't say that anymore.

Cory: *laughing harder.* What if I do, Tonto? Are you going to chop me with your tomahawk?

The other students look at them, but no one moves to stop Cory.

Len: *in a loud, clear voice.* I want you to stop saying that now.

Ms. Patel: *hearing the commotion, moves to Len's seat.* I heard what you said, Len. What's the problem?

Len: Sorry for being loud, Ms. Patel. But I'd like to handle this myself.

Cory, leery of calling attention to his behavior and fearing consequences from the teacher, slinks back to his seat. Len promises himself that from now on, every time Cory spews out his nasty names, he will tell him in a forceful manner to stop it.

In this instance, Len was able to stop the bullying before it got out of control. And he decided that if it did, he'd talk to his counselor about it. He knew from conversations with his family that no one should ever have to tolerate prejudice or abusive treatment.

He also knew, from an anti-bullying assembly his school sponsored, that strong, to-the-point replies can sometimes repel a bully. If they don't, it's time to tell a school counselor or administrator.

Tell When You Have To

Here's another example of responding to a bully, this time involving two fifth-grade girls, Madison and Kayla, waiting to catch the school bus.

Madison drops a ten-dollar bill on the ground and searches in the grass for it.

Moving swiftly, Kayla, a classmate, finds the bill under a rock and retrieves it. Dangling the bill above Madison, Kayla asks, "Were you looking for this?"

"You found it! Thanks," Madison says.

Kayla smiles slyly. "Finders keepers."

"You're keeping it?" Madison asks.

Kayla waves the ten in front of Madison's face. "Come and get it."

Madison reaches for the ten, and Kayla smacks her hard in the face, leaving a mark. Madison starts to cry.

"Crybaby," Kayla taunts.

The bus arrives, and Madison gets on, trying hard to hold in her tears so the other children don't notice.

Kayla follows her and says, "Don't tell or you'll be sorry."

Thinking about Kayla's reputation for bullying other kids, Madison knows it won't help to respond to her.

Before lunch, when Kayla is out of sight, Madison asks the teacher for a pass to see the counselor. Since Kayla used physical force, the counselor refers her case directly to Mr. Morgan, the principal.

Madison reluctantly tells the principal about Kayla not giving back her money and slapping her, expressing fear that Kayla will try to get back at her. She's witnessed Kayla hitting another girl before.

The principal reassures Madison that she will do everything she can to be sure that Kayla doesn't find the chance to get even.

Mr. Morgan calls Kayla into his office and suspends her from school for three days. When she brings in her parents to reinstate her, they tell the principal that Kayla will apologize to Madison and give back her money.

If she ever bothers Madison or any of the other girls, she will face consequences from home, such as grounding, no TV, or no going out with friends.

Her parents make it clear that they will act stricter in dealing with their child's actions so there won't be a repeat performance.

In this case, Madison used her common sense and did not wait to tell. She knew from talking to her parents and from discussions about bullying in her class that when bullying turns physical, you never wait to tell an adult. It's time to take action.

The counselor asked the parties involved (both sets of parents, plus Madison and Kayla) to meet for a restorative conference. If, as in this case, all parties (the bullied, the bully, and possibly the parents) are willing to listen and work to solve the problem, the counselor may want to call for a restorative conference to get the parties together to determine the problem and try to find a resolution.

In the following weeks, Kayla met with her counselor to discuss positive ways to relate to her classmates. Her parents cooperated by complimenting Kayla when the school issued positive behavior reports. They were willing to impose firm consequences if they heard that she was causing trouble, which she never did again. Because all parties cooperated, the restorative conference served as a helpful vehicle to put an end to the bullying.

Get Inside a Bully's Head

Trying to figure out what's inside a bully's head is no easy task. But even at a very young age, your child can predict with some degree of accuracy what motivates the bully he's dealing with and how to go about solving his specific problem. To do this, he has to use his best instincts and, of course, good old horse sense.

When your child approaches you with a bullying dilemma, you may want to ask her what she thinks this particular bully's goal is, to what degree and how often the person bullies, and how she and other kids react to the bullying.

One way of reinforcing this way of thinking is to ask her to write a character sketch of the bully (a brief composite of how she perceives the bully, what she does to bother your child and other kids, and what might work in getting the bully to stop what she's doing).

Some children (particularly younger ones) like to draw rather than write. If this holds true for your child, then have him draw a picture or stick figure of the person bothering him and write brief, descriptive words that characterize the bully.

In a way, trying to figure out a bully to know how to deal with him is like playing detective. Sometimes false leads that may cause the investigator to get sidetracked in wrong directions mysteriously pop up. The same holds true for trying to read a bully.

Ultimately, however, as in police work, the more adeptly your child learns to read people, the more of an advantage she holds in triumphing over the bully. This all translates into the importance of helping your children develop their instinctual impressions of people and events, especially as it applies to bullying.

Of course, your child may need your assistance and that of other adults to help with his problem, but meanwhile, trying to figure out where a bully's coming from and how to approach a problem caused by that mindset can provide your child with a helpful starting point for how to proceed with the bully.

Here's another incident that underscores the importance of your child's knowing how to use common sense to figure out what's going on inside the bully's brain.

Lamont, a burly third grader in the neighborhood, has taken on as his main pastime bothering Jamal, a first grader in a private school. Jamal, a short, slim, soft-spoken young man, who loves to create his own superhero comic books, wants Lamont to stop teasing him about his appearance. He's not sure of how to go about it until one day he comes up with a plan.

Jamal and his mother, Monique, are shopping at the mall for his birthday gift. Lamont and his friend Troy walk by them on the way to the food court.

Lamont bellows one of his pet names for Jamal. "Hey, Munchkin. You'd better get yourself a couple of pizzas and some fries so you put weight on that skimpy body."

Troy laughs. "I see why they call you 'Fun Size.' You are one tiny kid."

Monique stifles the urge to say something, but Jamal looks at them with a serious expression and addresses them in a loud voice. "I'm okay the way I am, so stop bugging me."

"Whoa, tiny tot, sorry. Didn't mean to rattle you. See you around, okay?" Lamont says. He and Troy headed toward the fast-food counter nudging one another.

A couple of days later, Lamont catches up with Jamal as he rides his bike with his older brother Willie on the street where they both live.

"Trying to make the marathon, Pygmy?" Lamont flexes his biceps. "You know you'll never be as good as me, so don't even try."

Jamal stops and looks at Lamont. With a straight face he says, "Thanks for saying that."

Befuddled by Jamal's response, Lamont frowns and walks away.

When Jamal and his brother get home, Willie tells their mother how Jamal bamboozled the bully with his "weird" response.

Monique smiled. "Is that the youngster we saw at the mall? I'm glad you said something to him that day. And now you've done it again. Nice job, son."

From the time her sons entered kindergarten, Monique has taken the time to talk to them in case they encountered a bully like Lamont. They'd discussed when to say something to a bully and when to ask for help.

Monique had talked with the boys about how to read clues on people's faces and watch the way they moved and spoke to them and others. Then, they were better able to know how to react when a bully crossed their paths.

In this case, even though Lamont was physically bigger than Jamal, he didn't perceive Lamont as a threat, so his first instinct was to try to handle the teasing himself. After a few snappy replies to his taunts, Lamont let up.

Apparently, the payoff wasn't big enough for Lamont to continue the teasing because Jamal didn't act upset about it. Lamont's goal of getting Jamal to cry was unattainable, so he backed off. All along, however, Jamal knew that if the teasing intensified or didn't stop, he'd be better off telling an adult. He wouldn't hesitate to do so if he thought it was the best course of action.

Use Facial Expressions and Body Movements to Boost Words

Jamal used a deadpan facial expression in his reply to Lamont. This helped get the intended result in that he used his face to drive home the message that he wasn't about to take Lamont's heckling anymore and that it wasn't going to change how he thought about himself. Because he and his mom had practiced using facial expressions and body motions to their best advantage beforehand, he remembered the importance of using these techniques in making his message meaningful.

It's not enough for your child to say something to the bully. She has to use her face and body movements to their best advantage to reinforce the message she wants the bully to take away. If she's shy, you'll want to practice at home by pretending you're the bully and asking her to reply with a one-liner and appropriate facial expressions and body language to give her message more punch.

When using facial expressions, it would help for your child to keep his face as neutral as possible without giving the bully a clue about what he's thinking. The name of the game is "keep the bully guessing." If the bully thinks you're smarter than he is, he may think twice before provoking you again.

Your child should avoid body movements such as shifting feet, blinking eyes, excessive hand-to-face movements, or looking downward, as the bully may interpret them as a lack of self-confidence or weakness.

In other words, your child should give the appearance of strength and mental toughness without seeming aggressive and combative, which may incite the bully further. This balance may not be easy to strike, but in some cases, it can prove advantageous in deterring a bully.

Of course, there will be occasions when your child may not see the need to talk to the bully at all. You'll want to make it clear to her that if she senses an immediate danger or if verbal replies coupled with facial and body movements aren't working, it's time to let a school authority know.

Hopefully, by this time, your child has already told you about the bullying, and you've both discussed it to see which path to pursue. Let him know that you expect him to keep you informed every step of the way.

Here's a girl who bolstered her words with body language in hopes of warding off a bully. Consider whether talking to the bully, paired with strong body language, work in this case.

Meet Raquel, an eighth grader in Eastern Middle, an inner-city public school, who takes pride in achieving good grades. A couple of her classmates, led by Luz, consider that a totally uncool thing to do and dog her constantly in the hallways of her crowded school.

Luz, a classmate who often faces suspension for cutting classes and defying teachers, calls Raquel names and threatens her whenever she gets the chance. Luz's friends take their orders from her and join in the harassment when Luz is around, but otherwise, they leave her alone. The girls in Luz's inner circle fear repercussions from her if they don't follow her lead.

Because of the noise level and teeming stream of students in the hallways at Eastern Middle, her tormenters enjoy a certain level of anonymity. Teachers, hall monitors, and administrators can't always get a clear view of everything that's going on as they try to keep the traffic flow moving and deal with more serious issues, such as fires in trash cans, students sparring verbally and physically, and potential drug deals.

Luz: cornering Raquel in the hallway. Hey, girl. You're getting on everyone's nerves, so stop playing teacher's pet. You're making it hard for the rest of us to pass when you act like Miss Smarty Pants.

Raquel: standing straight and talking firmly but quietly. I don't see how that should bother anybody.

Luz: lunging toward her. Me and my girls are sick of hearing about how great you are. Matter of fact, it's making me want to smack you around, teach you a lesson.

Raquel: backing away from her. Look, Luz. I'm not doing anything to bother you and your friends, so leave me alone. You do your thing and I'll do mine.

Luz: You're telling me what to do?

Raquel: speaking in a firm voice. I'm saying I don't want you to bother me anymore.

Luz: pushing Raquel forcefully up against a locker and banging her head. Nobody talks to me that way, so get that in your brainy skull.

Raquel pushes past her and races down the hall to her next class. She waits until after class to ask her teacher for a pass to the counselor so that Luz won't know that she's going to discuss what happened in the hallway.

In this case, Raquel used her common sense and told her counselor about Luz's threats and constant badgering in the hallways and about this more-recent physical attack. The counselor informed the principal, who reported the physical attack to the police.

The counselor also told her parents so that they could keep in touch with the school to help ensure that there were no further incidents.

Raquel tried using assertive speech and body language, but when that didn't work, she knew she had to take the next step and tell the counselor. As soon as Luz became more aggressive with her words and used physical force, she knew it was beyond her power to solve the problem on her own.

Consider Your Audience When Making a Joke

Some people say that trying to lighten things up in a tense situation will make things easier. That all depends on the way the bully is bothering your child and on how the bully thinks and reacts. Remind your child to use common sense in deciding whether to use humor to deter a bully.

If the bullying manifests itself as physical or psychological damage to your child or persists, she needs to tell you and the folks at school promptly. On the other hand, if the bullying is a sporadic or one-time occurrence, or if your child doesn't think it's of major consequence, then she may want to try coming back at the bully with a joke.

How does using common sense come into play when considering a jocular response to bullying? One thing to consider is the personality of the bully. If the person bothering your child has a heavy personality and people view him as negative and antagonistic, humor would be a bad move.

On the other hand, if the bully has been known to have moments when he has accepted a laugh at his own expense, he may be a good candidate for a funny comeback.

Here's the story of two friends. One decides to call the other names. Can the boy who's experiencing the teasing stop the bullying by using humor?

Matt and Logan are two third graders and longtime friends. One day at recess in the middle of shooting baskets, Logan starts showing off in front of the kids on the playground. He calls Matt a "klutz" and a "spaz," Logan's way of saying that he's uncoordinated and can't make a basket.

Matt: stops shooting baskets and looks at Logan. Really? I thought I was next in line for an NBA pick.

Logan: In your dreams, doofus. You can't even make the playground team.

Matt: laughing. I'm just having an off day. You know I can beat you at one-on-one anytime.

Logan: smiling. Pretty confident, aren't you? Okay, let's see what happens. *He throws Matt the ball and they start shooting baskets.*

In this instance, Matt attempts to diffuse the annoyance he feels when Logan calls him names. He also senses from the way they're looking at Logan that the kids around them feel uncomfortable, especially since Logan usually doesn't behave that way.

In fact, one of them shouted to Logan, "That's dumb. Knock it off." Another friend witnessing the heckling said, "Hey, friends don't say that to friends."

Mainly, Matt felt that making a lighthearted remark to Logan would probably bring his name-calling to an end. He also knew that this behavior was uncharacteristic of Logan, who usually acts like a good friend and a polite kid.

When Matt's friends who were present remarked negatively about Logan's name-calling, it also gave him reason to stop and think about how foolish his actions appeared to others. In all bullying events, the active role of friends and bystanders in coming to the victim's aid can greatly help deter a bully from harming another child.

After making a joke, Matt challenges Logan to a one-on-one, and they both get caught up in their game, diffusing what could have turned into a hurtful scene for Matt. Nevertheless, Matt promises himself that if Logan ever calls him names again, he will say something firm to him and let him know he won't stand for it.

Now, let's listen in on a conversation between two seventh graders in a magnet school for academically talented girls. Lilly, a cheerleader, has started calling Anna, the chess-team captain, offensive names because she thinks Anna's conceited due to her intelligence and the fact that she won the student-council election.

In truth, Anna works hard for her grades and enjoys popularity and respect among her classmates for her caring and sincere nature. Lilly's names for Anna include "anorexic," "bulimic," and "mummy," all of which upset her because she is self-conscious about her slender body, which is not due to problem eating habits, but to genetics.

Lilly accosts Anna in the bathroom after school when most of the staff has left.

Lilly: pointing her finger near Anna's face. Hey, skinny bitch, when are you going to stop being such a kiss up in class?

Anna: I don't like those names.

Lilly: eyes narrowing and arms crossed. Well, isn't that too bad. The fact is you look like a corpse, and everybody thinks you're a dog.

Anna: Better being a slim dog than an overweight one. You won't have to use your pooper scooper as much.

Lilly: What's that supposed to mean?

Anna: Because the dog doesn't eat much, it won't have to go to the bathroom as much.

Lilly: Don't try to change the subject with your stupid jokes. Be warned. We're going to post your scrawny body in that bikini you wore to the class swim party all over the Internet if you don't stop making the rest of us look dumb in class.

Without responding, Anna walks out of the bathroom at a brisk pace, leaving Lilly to apply her pound of makeup.

In this example, Anna tried joking with Lilly, but she saw that she couldn't change Lilly's angry, aggressive attitude. In fact, the joke seemed to inflame Lilly more. When Lilly threatened Anna, she knew she had to leave the scene of the bullying. Once she felt threatened, she wasted no time in vacating the bathroom.

Because of the heightening viciousness of Lilly's taunts and the threat of posting her picture on the Internet, Anna knew that she could not try a humorous response with her again. After the incident, Anna wondered if she'd acted properly in responding to her at all since Anna's tone was vicious and her body language (pointing at her face, eyes narrowing, arms crossed) reflected her growing rage.

If the teasing intensified or persisted, Anna's next step would be to talk to her mother and the school headmistress and to develop a plan to make Lilly stop the teasing, which had turned into outright harassment on this occasion.

Stay Out of Harm's Way

Anna's encounter with Lilly in the girls' bathroom underscores the point that your children need to be aware at all times of where they are and where the bully is. Had she thought about it, she might have opted to leave the scene immediately when she spotted her nemesis. Or if she'd known that Lilly's pattern was to use the bathroom to apply her makeup at that time every day, she might have chosen not to go in at all.

Help your child become aware of the sights, sounds, and feelings evident in places he frequents. Often we are able to sense that something is not right when we enter a certain location. And when we find ourselves in that situation, where danger may be imminent, it's best not to stay there and take a chance of something happening.

Avoid making your child overly cautious and fearful, but caution him to use instincts to pick up on people and places that may present a danger to him. If he feels unsafe for any reason, he should leave the area at once. Better to err on the side of caution than to make himself vulnerable to mistreatment and abuse.

It's not as far-fetched to think about a bully's particular ways of operating, patterns of daily activity, and places he frequents on a regular basis as some may think.

People are often predictable, and, if someone's after you, it pays to know what they're up to and places they go to on a regular basis.

If the bully's been known to frequent a certain location within the school or neighborhood or if your child finds herself alone, she needs to exercise caution. Tell her to stay around friends if she absolutely has to be in a place where she might encounter trouble.

Naturally, there are some locations your children can't possibly avoid, such as the school or public bus, the classroom, the locker room, the hallways, and the school yard. But they can be alert about how to avoid their pursuers in these locations.

For example, if trouble lurks on the school bus, your child should make it a point to sit up front near the bus driver and to share a seat with a friend. If the driver assigns seats, you or your child can talk to the driver privately and explain why she needs a front seat.

Public buses and subway stops provide an environment for bullying activities to thrive, as security in these areas is often limited or nonexistent. Sometimes, schools assign security to these areas, but they're often short on supervision, and bullies grab the chance to attack their targets. Bullies can easily assault their victims without anyone finding out until the damage is done.

Another place to watch is the locker room. If your child needs to be in the gym locker room after school hours, he should be sure there are others around rather than take a chance on meeting up with the bully. The hidden nooks and valleys in these areas can induce a bully to corner victims without fear of someone witnessing it.

Do you remember Luz, who pushed Raquel against her locker in the hallway? Hallways are an ideal place for bullies to stalk and badger their targets because of the noise and anonymity factor, particularly when children move to the cafeteria or recess or race to change classes.

The school yard during recess is a common place for bullying in elementary schools, as teachers can't give their full attention to everything that's going on simultaneously. Also, in middle schools before and after school, bullies can work their mischief by hiding out on the school campus and taking victims by surprise.

Let's observe how Khaleed, a middle-school student and potential member of the basketball team, handles a potential bullying episode in the gym locker. Ever since the start of the school year when Khaleed moved to this country with his physician parents, two boys, Wyatt and Blake, have ridiculed him by calling him names such as "foreigner" and "illegal alien," telling him to go back to his place of birth because he isn't "a real American."

Khaleed tried talking to them, but it only made them pester him more. Finally, after conferring with his parents, he went to his counselor, Ms. Greene, who informed the assistant principal that the two boys were tormenting him.

Today, Khaleed is heading to the gym locker to prepare for basketball tryouts. Wyatt and Blake spot him in the hallway after school on his way to tryouts.

Wyatt: Go back where you came from. We don't want you here.

Blake: eyeing the gym bag and basketball he's carrying. You're actually going to try out for our team?

Khaleed doesn't reply.

Wyatt: It's a known fact that people from your country can't play sports. So why even try?

Blake: What you should do is transfer out of here to one of those religious schools your people go to so we won't have to look at you.

Still not responding, Khaleed hurries toward the gym.

The boys race to catch up with him. Khaleed, seeing that he's the only other student in the gym area, calmly turns around and walks toward the school office. Wyatt and Blake shout after him.

Wyatt: Where do you think you're going, you little wuss? Now I guess you'll lose your chance to make the team. Not that you would have a chance. *They both laugh and go back to the gym.*

Blake: calling after him. You can't escape us. We'll find you and once we do, we'll get you.

Khaleed goes to the counselor's office and talks to Ms. Greene, who tells him that she'll inform the coach of Wyatt and Blake's latest attempts at intimidation.

When the coach finds out, he benches Wyatt and Blake until they promise never to bother Khaleed again. Although they don't apologize, their passion to play basketball supersedes their inclination to bully Khaleed. They stop calling him names, but they still glower at him in the halls and in class, which hardly fazes Khaleed, given what he's been through with them.

Khaleed used his common sense in dealing with Wyatt and Blake in that he informed his counselor once he felt he needed outside help. He also knew that talking to them wouldn't help and would probably worsen the problem.

Therefore, he made the choice to leave the scene where more vicious bullying had the potential to play out. The halls were deserted, and two against one was something he didn't feel prepared to deal with, especially since he weighed half as much as Wyatt, also a fullback on the neighborhood football team.

Also, very often, contacting a coach or activity sponsor first can help a situation like this in which the stakes are high for the bully to stop intimidating a victim. If that didn't work, the counselor would have immediately contacted the administration. But in this instance, the counselor knew the boys involved and felt that this would be a better route to take.

What if your child has tried everything possible to put off the bully and nothing has helped despite your talks, advice, and role-playing sessions? Would you know how to navigate the school system if you had to take the next step? Suppose your school was not as receptive as you would like to your requests to work with you to stop a bully from bothering your child?

How can you act as your child's advocate to make the school system more receptive to the bullying problems that plague your child? How can you work one-on-one with school personnel to ensure your child's safety? And if that doesn't work, what can you do? Where can you go for help?

That is the scope of chapter 7, "Know How to Navigate the System."

KEY POINTS: Chapter 6

- Advise your children to use their instincts to determine if the teasing is serious.
- Advise your children not to talk to a bully if there's a chance it would place them in physical or psychological danger.
- If your children decide to talk to a bully, suggest that they use as few words as possible and speak clearly and firmly.
- Discuss ways of predicting things about the bully's behavior to help your children come up with a good solution to the problem.
- Practice using facial expressions and body language to boost words.
- Remind your children to keep the bully guessing.
- Advise your children to give the appearance of strength and mental toughness without seeming aggressive and combative.
- If your children sense an immediate danger or if verbal replies and facial and body language don't work, they should inform the school authorities.
- Coming back at the bully with a joke is something your children may want to try if the bullying is sporadic or seems like a one-time occurrence.
- Tell your children to be aware of a bully's particular ways of operating, patterns of daily activity, and places he or she frequents on a regular basis.

CHAPTER SEVEN

~

Know How to Navigate the System

Form a Partnership with Your School

How serious is bullying in our schools? To answer that question, look at the newspapers and TV. You'll read about a growing number of children committing suicide because bullies literally taunted them to death.

You'll read the story of a young man who killed himself because of bullying. Some of his peers had the nerve to write homophobic hate messages on his Facebook memorial page, continuing to bully the victim after his death.

You'll hear about the bullies who attended a bullied child's funeral. They approached the body and laughed at the girl because of the way she looked after she had died by committing suicide. What types of people could show such a total lack of empathy?

These are the kinds of individuals we're dealing with. We don't know the reason they act this way. Maybe they were brought up to act in antisocial ways by inadequate role models. Possibly, the electronic world that dominates our lives fuels a lack of concern for their fellow students as human beings, and they see them as objects rather than people with feelings.

Or could it be that bullies are amoral beings who don't know or care about how they hurt other humans? None of these possible reasons matter. What does matter is the fact that our children come in contact with bullies every day, and their main goal is to harm innocent victims and to dehumanize them in the process.

That is why you need to deal with your child's bullying problem head-on and to work until you find a solution to her bullying dilemma.

Stopping a bully is hard work. Sometimes you'll need to enlist the help of school staff to help your child in dealing with a stubborn or recurring bullying issue. Mainly, you are the primary person who needs to be in constant touch with your child every time a bullying problem occurs. If communication remains constant and meaningful between you and your child, by the time a problem surfaces, you'll be ready to act on it in a timely and effective way.

Some parents hesitate speaking to teachers and administrators about any concerns, thinking they will label them as pests who question their every move about the curriculum, grading system, and school disciplinary policies. A few parents fear that teachers will take it out on their children if they ask questions and express their views about what goes on in school.

Granted, it's important to strike a balance between genuine concerns about policies affecting your children and letting the staff do their job of teaching your children.

On the other hand, when serious bullying problems arise, it's imperative to initiate a partnership between you, your child, and the school to begin solving the problem. Your child and you cannot do it alone. You need to form an alliance with your school in which all parties work together to eliminate bullying.

That's why it's smart to speak up and let teachers and administrators know that you want the staff to become more aware of bullying as it concerns your school in general and your child in particular. You'll also want them to keep you promptly informed of any bullying issues your child encounters.

Be sure to keep a dated record of any contacts you have with teachers and administrators in writing, so that should you need to seek help from higher levels of the school administration, you can document what you've already done. Include in your record the name of the person you spoke to, what was said, what was done, and any concerns you have along the way.

Attend School Board Meetings

School board meetings are a perfect forum for bringing your concerns to the public about how the school system deals with bullying as it involves your child, and possibly other people's children.

Attending these meetings will give you and other parents the chance to air your opinions about the district's bullying policy and its enforcement. Because the press is always a fixture at these meetings, which are sometimes televised, you will reap the added benefit of gaining publicity for your cause.

Should you decide to speak, present your case as clearly and concisely as possible, using the records you've kept when dealing with the school and/

or central office. You may want to start by relating a bullying episode that recently occurred and speak about your degree of satisfaction with how the school handled it.

However, if you believe that the school didn't take care of the problem properly, state what you want done and why it is important to all parents in the district that the school board follows through on it. Request a follow-up report of the members' findings at the next meeting, which you and other parents will attend.

In line with this, make an effort to organize supporters whose children may also find themselves coping with bullying. Urge these parents to attend school board meetings and recommend that they discuss their suggestions for remedying bullying problems in your district.

In addition to voicing your opinions and asking questions about how the district is handling bullying, you'll want to encourage your district to use the federal and state funds made available to promote bully prevention programs in a way that will best benefit the children.

Ask What Your School Is Doing to Combat Bullying

Getting closer to home, you can ask your school principal or assistant principal how these federal and state programs show up in your school. Are they made an integral part of the curriculum rather than showing up as part of a monthly assembly program or a brief sound byte delivered over the PA system?

Ask teachers, students, and administrators about students' reactions to the assemblies. Do students tend to take them seriously, or do they dismiss them as another boring school assembly?

In some schools where bullying is rampant, students have joked about such programs. If this is the case, ask the principal what can be done to stress the fact that bullying is not only hurtful but also lethal to many children. Ask what you and other parents can do to help reinforce this message. Do the programs work across the curriculum by incorporating curricular goals in all of the major subject areas?

For example, in language arts class, teachers can reinforce speaking skills by staging panel discussions about bullying. They can work on writing skills by having students journal about bullying incidents they've experienced or witnessed. Some students can share what they've observed with the class.

In social studies class, students can discuss what the state and federal governments have done in the area of bully-prevention programs to support local school systems. In health classes, students can role-play bullying situations and discuss what they as individuals can do to combat bullying in their schools and communities.

Here are other questions to discuss with your school administrator: Do all of the students understand why bullying is wrong and know what to say if a bully bothers them? Do they know whom to turn to for help? If a bully disturbs their peace of mind, do they know how to articulate this to a counselor or administrator?

It would be helpful for you and other parents to learn about your state's anti-bullying laws. You can access the Web at bullypolice.org to learn the latest information about these laws.

You can also ask your representative to help you access them. Once you learn about these laws and the anti-bullying policies of your school district, find out how your district enforces them.

If you find that these laws and policies are not being applied, then contact the central administration of your district and express your concerns. And ask for answers. You can say something like this: "I'm aware that there's a zero tolerance policy for bullying in our district. However, someone shoved my child on the school bus and the district did nothing about it. How can you help me remedy this situation?"

Use the words "How can you help me?" whenever you can, as the people in charge are more likely to respond to them rather than something more intimidating such as: "What are you going to do about it?" If you insert the word *me* in your request, it personalizes it and makes the people you're talking to aware that you're asking them to be accountable to you personally.

If they say they're working on implementing the policy but that it takes time, stay in touch until you get a specific answer about how they plan to intervene. Be polite, but be persistent. Tell them you want a timeline of the actions they plan to take and that you'll be in contact with them in what you consider to be a fair amount of time to learn about what they're doing to rectify the situation.

Get to Know Teachers, Counselors, and Administrators

Although you'll want to make yourself known at school board meetings and to school administrators, it's equally, if not more, useful to get to know your child's teachers, counselors, and administrators.

They are the first line of defense against bullying, the professionals most likely to see how the bully is acting toward your child and how your child reacts when the bully confronts him. Add the school nurse to that list. Often, after a bullying episode, the teacher will send the victim to the nurse, or the child will end up there on his own.

To get an idea of how you can approach your child's teacher about a bullying problem, listen in on a phone conversation between Alicia's fourth-grade teacher, Mr. Torres, and Alicia's mother, Rachel. Alicia is a shy, developmentally delayed student in an inclusion class in a public elementary school. Three of her classmates ridicule her speech and the fact that she's very small for her age.

Rachel: Thanks for calling me back, Mr. Torres. I guess you can tell from our last conversation how upset I am that those kids haven't let up on Alicia.

Mr. Torres: We're working on it, Ms. Konzyk, but these things take time. We're doing everything we can.

Rachel: I appreciate that, but we need to do more. I'm hoping you can help me by coming up with a specific plan. I want to know what kind of day she's having on a regular basis. I'd like you to give me a report at the end of each school day, stating what you've observed in terms of the kids bullying her.

Mr. Torres: I'd like to help you, Ms. Konzyk, but it would be difficult to do what you're asking. If I had to monitor every student's interactions with peers, I wouldn't have time to teach. That is not to say I'm not keeping on top of things. How about if I call you every Friday to let you know how it's going?

Rachel: That would help, but here's a way you can let me know how things go each day. You know those daily report forms you give children if they're having trouble in a subject or behavior in your class, the ones the parents have to initial each day and send back to school after the teacher gives a brief report on subject and behavior?

Mr. Torres: nodding. Sure, but those forms don't leave room for detailed reports about other matters, such as bullying. I don't have time to write a full report every time someone teases Alicia. But I will do what I can to help.

Rachel: I understand that. But all you'd have to do is initial "S" or "U" for "satisfactory" or "unsatisfactory," which would mean you think things are going well or that you think there's a reason for more intervention on my part or the school's. If I see a "U," I'll know it's time to talk to you and the principal.

Mr. Torres: I think that would be doable. I'll start the daily report tomorrow. If the bullying gets worse, or if I feel that we need more help, I'll indicate that with an "unsatisfactory." If everything seems to be going well, I'll write "satisfactory." And meanwhile, I'll talk to the counselor and the principal about continuing to meet with the three girls involved in the bullying.

I know that the principal has a conference tomorrow with the ringleader's parents.

Rachel: Thanks, Mr. Torres. I'll be in touch. It's very important to me and Alicia's father that our daughter feels comfortable in school. We want to see an end to her mistreatment now.

Mr. Torres: I'll do whatever I can to help.

Every day but one the following week, Mr. Torres wrote an "S" in the daily report. On Friday, when he wrote a "U," Rachel called for an appointment and spoke to the principal about intensifying the consequences for the children bothering Alicia. In Rachel's view, the teasing had degenerated into cruelty.

That Friday, Alicia said that she didn't want to go to school ever again because the girls who were bothering her called her "dummy," "dwarf," and "freak." They told her she shouldn't have been born.

The principal said that after the parental conference that Monday before, the girls had stopped bothering Alicia. However, on Friday, she got a report from Mr. Torres that the bullying had started up again and had become more malicious.

At that point, she suspended the ringleader and her sidekick. The principal made it clear that she was going to tell the parents at the reinstatement conference that if the bullying continued, she'd recommend transfer of their children to an alternative school, which targets kids with discipline problems.

The parents of the girls thought these were pretty stiff consequences, but, by then, the bullying had been going on for a couple of months, and the tone of it was becoming more hateful.

Rachel was pleased with how the daily report worked and how swiftly the school moved in implementing her suggestion. The fact that she'd let the teacher know that she appreciated his help resonated with him, and he, in turn, became more responsive to her ideas. She also listened to his point of view before giving her opinion about how to proceed.

After she did these things, she added her suggestion and found him more receptive than he might have been had she approached him as an adversary. She believed he wanted to help, and she wanted to encourage him further in that direction.

If the school hadn't moved fast in solving the problem, she would have gone to the next level, which, in her district, was the director of elementary education.

Make it a point to learn the chain of command in your school district. If one person doesn't help you, then it's time to contact the next person in the school hierarchy. If you don't know who that person is, the principal or the district personnel office will have that information.

If you're not satisfied with the way the school is handling the problem, tell the principal, calmly but assertively, that you will go to the next level if you have to. Sometimes, letting the administration know that you're not going away until they resolve the problem will help hasten action on their part.

Once you know your school district's structure, you'll know where to go for help should you need it. Keep in mind that city school systems often contain more administrative levels than suburban schools because of their size.

Whatever school district you belong to, the final rung in the ladder is the school board. Once again, keep a dated anecdotal record of any contacts you have in your school system. Keep a record of how you perceived your dealings with each staff member along the way so that you can document your interactions should you need to approach the next level of school administration.

If you don't find satisfaction within the system itself, you may want to contact the school board president in writing or request an appointment. Of course, all of this takes time, which you probably don't have when your child is facing a bullying problem. That's why it's best to try first to handle your problem at the school level. If that doesn't work, you may have no choice.

Most teachers and administrators are willing to help, especially if you can offer specific suggestions as Rachel did when talking to the teacher. As in the other examples throughout this book, simple solutions that employ common sense often prove to be the most helpful.

Hail, Hail, the Gang's All Here

There is strength in numbers, and if you know how to get the gang (all the people in the school community) on your side, then you're one step ahead in your goal of helping your child say, "Bye-bye bullies."

Another group of people whose acquaintance you'll want to make at school includes office personnel, nonteaching assistants, and custodians. You may wonder how getting to know these people who aren't involved directly in teaching your children can help you in your goal of saving your child from the bully's clutches.

The truth is that the more people around your child each day that you involve in your child's life, the more they will watch out for her and be willing to help if they sense danger for her.

The head secretary is often the first person who will talk to your child if he goes to see the principal about a bullying issue. You may want to fill in the secretary about what's going on so that she can be aware of the situation and help by making sure your child gets priority in seeing the principal whenever he needs to rather than waiting for an appointment.

Additionally, nonteaching assistants, or classroom aides, often come into close contact with your child more than the teacher does. The aide gets to know your child because he often works with small groups in the classroom and can closely observe the students' interactions.

The aide sees the little exchanges that sometimes go unnoticed by the teacher as kids work in their cooperative learning groups. She's also privy to how they sometimes exclude or throw digs at another student. The aide has a better opportunity to observe what goes on in large-group instruction when the teacher is giving a lesson. She may hear unkind remarks or laughter about a certain student or may observe someone poking, pushing, or tripping a classmate.

For these reasons, you will want to talk to classroom aides and ask that they contact you if they notice any problems your child faces with bullying that the teacher may have missed or is too busy to notice. Tell the aide that you won't require a lot of time but that you'd appreciate a brief phone call to the counselor, who will, in turn, contact you if someone bothers your child. Then you can quickly contact the school and follow up before the incident veers out of control.

Another helpful resource in your efforts to protect your child from bullies is the school custodian. You can find the custodian in hallways, classrooms, the cafeteria, and bathrooms, fixing broken windows or restoring heat or coolness to the building. Sometimes the custodian will be working outside the building when students file out of school buses or walk into the building when the bell rings.

The fact that the custodian doesn't stay in one place for very long and eventually comes into contact with the entire student body gives him the chance to get to know kids in a different way from teachers or administrators.

Some children make friends with the school custodian and confide in her more than they would a teacher or assistant principal whom they view mainly as an authority figure. For this reason, you may find it advantageous to introduce yourself to the custodian if your child is subjected to bullying. Ask her if she sees anything you should know about to contact the counselor, who will forward the information to you. In most cases, any staff members, including custodians, will be happy to oblige.

Have you ever thought about contacting parents of your child's friends or classmates who are dealing with bullying? It may help you to exchange ideas and discuss what has and hasn't worked when bullies pestered your children.

Ask your child if any of his friends are being bullied. Talk to your neighbors and see if any of their children have dealt with bullying issues. Ask the parents of bullied children that you've made contact with if they'll back you when you need help, and tell them you're willing to reciprocate. Network with these parents informally, and keep in touch with them to work on problems and share victories.

Maybe you both have a child in the same school and find that the administration is slow in moving to solve the problem to your satisfactions. In that case, you may want to go together as a group to voice your concerns about what the school administration or the next level up is doing to help your children.

This is not to say that you'll band together like a group of vigilantes to intimidate the staff, but rather to make the point that the bullying problems in your school involve more than one child (yours) and that you all hope to work together with the administration to create a positive change for your children.

How will you know when your child is facing a bullying problem that affects her so profoundly that she must seek help immediately? How do you know when bullying is serious enough to warrant you or your child informing someone at school of the problems he's encountering? At what point should you go beyond the classroom teacher and counselor and seek the help of the building administrator? Beyond that, when should you start moving up the administrative ladder in search of help?

See chapter 8 for an in-depth look at these issues.

KEY POINTS: Chapter 7

- Your children need to be in constant touch with you every time a bullying problem occurs. You are the primary "go-to" person.
- Form an alliance with your school in which all parties work together to eliminate bullying.
- Speak up and let teachers and administrators know that you want the staff to become more aware of bullying as it concerns your school in general and your children in particular.
- Keep a dated record in writing of any contacts you have with teachers and administrators.
- Bring your concerns about bullying to the public at school board meetings.
- Ask your school administrator how federal and state programs show up in your school bully prevention program.
- Get to know your children's teachers, counselors, and administrators.
- Know the chain of command in your school district. If one person doesn't help you, then contact the next person in the school hierarchy.

CHAPTER EIGHT

~

Take Action When Your Child Is in Distress

Keep in Close Touch with Your Child

The title of this book implies that you will be the prime mover in protecting your child from bullies. However, if you've read between the lines, you've also seen that one of the main goals of this book is to help you help your child learn ways to cope when she encounters a bully. Ideally, you'll teach and reinforce those skills through discussions and role-playing so that your child will have an idea of how to help herself should she encounter a bully.

It's imperative that your child knows how to use common sense in dealing with a bully so that he feels confident in helping himself. It's equally important that your child keeps in close touch with you so that he can bounce ideas off you. He'll also need to feel comfortable talking to you when things get too tough to tolerate or too hard to handle on his own. That kind of rapport takes years to cultivate; that's why you'll want to work at building that trust every day from the very beginning.

Realistically, a bullying victim can't always handle things on her own, so you will be the one to stand by her, and, along with the school, assist her in dealing with problems bullies present. Even with minor bullying episodes, encourage your child to talk with you openly so that should things escalate or continue without the prospect of improving, your child will feel comfortable in turning to you for advice and support.

Once you've established that bond with your child that allows him to talk to you about anything, no matter how minor the bullying event may appear, you'll have a better chance of catching the problem in time to help.

Be Aware of Distress Signs in Your Child

Be sensitive of distress signs in your child so that you know when you'll have to act rapidly in a bullying situation. First and foremost, consider what your child's usual behavioral patterns are like.

For example, if she usually doesn't sleep a lot and suddenly starts sleeping until mid-day on the weekends, or if she likes going out with friends and suddenly starts sequestering herself in her room for hours, then it's time to start inquiring about what's causing her to act this way. This is not to say you need to prod and nag, which, as you know, will get you nowhere.

Basically, it's best to listen rather than talk and to ask open-ended, non-threatening questions such as "How were things at school today?" Another thing you can do is make simple observations about your child's behavior and wait for him to respond. You might say, "I can tell that something's bothering you today. What can I do to help?"

Of course, children, even our own, are often hard to read. And sometimes it's difficult to tell the difference between preteen and teenage angst and bona fide depression. Be aware, though, that one of the main hallmarks of depression is that it doesn't get better without some kind of intervention. It doesn't go away on its own.

However, you can look at your child and know if she is so far afield from the way she usually acts that you need to take action in the form of contacting the school, along with needing a psychological support system.

As an example of a child who has shown a significant personality change when bullied severely, we'll observe Les, a fifth grader in a suburban elementary school. His mother, Mary, has noticed Les behaving differently in the past few days. She hears Les getting up and roaming around the house all hours of the night, while all his life he was a sound sleeper.

She also notices that he's eating more sweets lately and has packed more weight onto his already overweight body. He's spending hours in his room with the door locked and refuses to do his homework. Although he has to struggle to maintain decent grades because of a learning problem, he always completes all his assignments and takes pride in getting A's for his class participation and homework.

What disturbs Mary most, however, is the fact that Les refuses to go to school. He says that he can't face the kids in his class because a few of them make fun of his name, "Leslie," calling it a girl's name. Worse than that, some kids he doesn't even know reinforce the bullying by chanting "Les is more" and "Grossness!" at him in the hallways and on the bus.

Some of the younger kids, taking cues from their older classmates, call him "fat boy" and "lard ass." A few make throw-up noises in the lunchroom when they see him in the food line. Some kids from his class also hurl their leftover food at him.

Mary has called the principal many times, but the bullying persists. Yesterday, the boy sitting behind him on the bus flicked him in the head with his fingernail and punched him on the shoulder. This time, Mr. Weiss, the principal, suspended the boy, but on the other occasions, he said there were so many kids involved in the hazing that he was having trouble making a positive identification.

Mr. Weiss knew that Les would never tell for fear he'd be subjected to fiercer treatment. In effect, he wanted to wait a while to see if, in time, the bullying would subside on its own as it sometimes did in other cases he'd handled. However, Les' mother was unwilling to take that chance. Because of the severity and length of Les' mistreatment, she knew that something had to be done in a hurry.

In the meantime, taking Les' counselor's advice, Mr. Weiss made plans for a bully-prevention assembly in which he would address the different types of bullying witnessed by school staff. He would not specifically focus on Les' case, as he did not want to inflame the bullies further, which he thought might worsen their treatment of Les. Mr. Weiss planned to conclude his presentation by promising serious consequences for all students who participated in bullying.

Mr. Mays, the school counselor, has been in constant touch with Les and his mother since the bullying began. When things become intolerable, he lets Les sit in his office to work on his assignments, but he tells Mary that it's only a temporary solution until the bullying abates.

Les gets to the point where he loses valuable class time, which is a problem. Because of his learning disability, he depends on the teacher's detailed explanations to help him do well in his tests.

To make matters worse, Les begins lashing out at his mother. Before the bullying started, he was always pleasant and polite to his parents, so this was a complete turnaround for him.

That night, Les' mother calls him for dinner, and when he doesn't show up at the table, she goes up to his room and raps on the locked door.

Les: sprawled across his bed. Go away.

Mary repeatedly knocks on the door, but Les refuses to open it.

Mary: unlocking the door with a skeleton key. Come down for dinner. Dad and your brother are waiting.

Les: Tell them I'm not hungry.

Mary: Come down and sit with us anyway.

Les: I don't want to.

Mary: sitting next to him on the bed and putting her hand on his shoulder. Look, Les, I know you're feeling pretty miserable about what's going on at school. Because this isn't getting any better, I have an appointment at the school's district office tomorrow. I'm going to see how they can help Mr. Weiss deal with this.

Les: frowning at her. If you hadn't named me "Leslie," it wouldn't have happened.

Mary: You know you were named after your grandfather. It's a name to be proud of, and no one should pick on you because of it.

Les: I also inherited the fat gene from you and Dad. That's why I can't stop gaining weight.

Mary: That may be part of it, but eating four candy bars and skipping dinner isn't helping. Anyway, your name and your weight don't give those kids permission to say nasty things to you. And they never have the right to lay their hands on you like that boy on the bus did.

Les: I can't change my name because I don't want to disrespect Grandpa, and I'll never lose weight. So I guess it's never going to stop.

Mary: You're right about the name, but I can help you with the weight. And you can help too, by coming down to dinner. If you eat the right things, then you won't want to stuff yourself on candy, no matter how much those kids upset you.

Les: Okay. I'll come down, but you know I hate fish—I can smell it from here—so don't ask me to eat it.

Mary: smiling. It so happens I have some leftover chicken from last night, your favorite.

Les: Leftovers, yuk.

Mary: And Les, I'm going to do everything I can to get the school to help. We can do it together.

Les: I don't ever want to go to school again.

Mary: You can't afford to keep losing class time, so the counselor is sending a classroom aide to sit in on your classes with you until this blows over. She'll sit in the back of the room so the kids won't know she's there to help you. If any kids bother you, the aide will make a note of it and let the principal know. It's only until we work things out, maybe a couple of days.

Les: I don't like that idea. It makes me look dumb, but I hate the way things are too, so I guess I have no choice. What about the lunchroom and the bus? They're the worst places.

Mary: I've talked to Ms. Curry, the bus driver, and she's giving you a front seat, where you can sit with your friend Chase. As for lunch, the counselor says you can eat in her office until this is settled. But don't touch that bowl of candy bars she keeps on her desk.

Les: rolling his eyes. You had to say that, didn't you?

Mary: Let's go downstairs. Can you hear Dad's stomach growling?

The next day, Mary and her husband, Luke, meet with the director of elementary education, along with the school security officer, at the district office. They devise a plan for identifying the ringleaders of the kids bothering Les.

Before Mr. Weiss holds the bully prevention assembly, he learns that the same small group of students that bullied Les is picking on other children. He promises strict consequences for anyone found bullying on the school grounds or on the bus.

Within a week, because of the principal's proclamation about consequences, the bullying of Les and the other students lessens significantly. No one dares bother Les because the principal has kept his promise by suspending the students who bullied him and the others.

Les' dark mood gradually lifts, and he starts to enjoy going to school and seeing some of his good friends again. With his mother's help, he starts eating healthy foods and begins an exercise program with his dad. When he starts to lose weight gradually, his confidence grows, and he tries out for the baseball team.

In Les' case, his mother could immediately determine that he had strayed from his usual pattern of behavior. Given that cue, she used her common sense and sprang into action, listening to what he had to say.

She also responded in an empathic way to his anger and sadness in the face of cruel treatment from some of his peers. Additionally, she elicited the help of the school, and she and her husband consulted the district office to see how they could help further.

Mary and Les' dad worked with Les to bolter his self-confidence by encouraging him to lose weight and to try out for the baseball team.

Due to Les' mother's quick response, Les, the school, and the district office joined forces to help Les see a positive end to a major bout with bullying.

Watch for Major Changes

Sometimes bullying affects a child so profoundly that it can precipitate major depression or suicide. Parents of children who have committed suicide have often reported frustration in getting the school to help them stop bullies from harassing their child. By the time anyone was willing to help, it was too late.

Many of these victims showed signs of personality changes before their deaths, such as withdrawal from family and friends; physical symptoms, such as headaches and stomachaches; changes in sleep or eating habits; and excessive crying. On the other hand, some showed no signs at all.

Some children refuse to go to school and isolate themselves from family members and friends. If your child talks to a family member or friend about death or mentions suicide, then there's a good chance he's in serious trouble and may be contemplating killing himself.

To assess the gravity of your child's mental state, you'll need to talk to her gently about how she's feeling mentally and physically. If your common sense tells you that something's not right, it's time to ask for professional help.

Be sure to contact the school counselor and the school administration to let them know how concerned you are and to insist that something is done immediately to correct the situation. If you're really worried and feel that you need help immediately, take your child to your local hospital for crisis evaluation, and professionals will determine the level of care needed.

Although Les, the bullying victim in our last example, experienced eating and sleeping problems, he was still at the point where he could communicate with his parents and cooperate to some degree in finding an answer to his problem. Though he sometimes acted out in an angry way at home, he continued to communicate with his parents and brother when they tried to talk with him about his problems at school.

The key here is that his symptoms did not markedly interfere with his life, and when they did, he was still able to cope to a degree that led his mother to believe that he had some measure of control over his emotional state.

If his mother had thought that he was seriously depressed, she most likely would have taken him to a psychologist right away. As it was, she monitored his state of mind carefully and determined that she and her husband would work with the school system to find an answer. If that answer were not imminent, she would then have sought professional help immediately.

Get All Parties Involved in a Major Case of Bullying

Although Les showed signs that the harassment was traumatic for him, De-Shawn, an eighth grader in an urban public middle school, exhibited a more severe reaction. His uncle and guardian, Anthony, was aware that DeShawn was being bullied by a few kids in his school due to their perceptions of his sexual orientation. Although he wasn't gay, he had a couple of gay friends that he hung out with regularly. The straight kids avoided him because they believed he was gay.

It started with a few kids in his gym class calling him "queer," "homo," and "fag," and ended with a couple of boys on the football team roughing him up in the lunchroom one afternoon.

The school nurse called his guardian to pick him up after administering first aid for his cuts and bruises. After the nurse reported the incident to Ms. Wilson, the principal, the principal told her that she'd make the school staff aware of the bullying and call in the boys responsible for the attack.

The principal had already viewed the security camera's identification of the perpetrators. Security promptly rounded them up and questioned them. At the same time, the school police were gathering evidence to arrest the boys for assault.

The next day, the school attendance officer informed Anthony, DeShawn's guardian, that DeShawn had not shown up for school. Before that day, Anthony noticed that his nephew had barely touched his breakfast and dinner and had spent most of his time in his room repeatedly playing the same song.

Anthony had heard the song before but didn't pay much attention to the lyrics. However, his instincts told him to take a moment to listen to the song. If DeShawn spent hours listening to it, there must be a reason he was drawn to it. When Anthony went up to DeShawn's room to hear the song, he was shaken to discover that the lyrics dealt with death by suicide.

Since DeShawn's parents had died a few years back in a car crash and Anthony had taken responsibility for him, his nephew had always confided in him. He knew all of his nephew's friends but wasn't aware of any enemies.

However, within the last couple of weeks, Anthony noticed that DeShawn had become more quiet and sullen. When Anthony heard him crying in his room one night and banged on his door, DeShawn refused to open it. Around that same time, the teacher called Anthony and spoke to him about how some students were calling him names and referred DeShawn to the counselor.

After all that had happened by this point, Anthony was certain that DeShawn was depressed, and possibly, suicidal. After the call from the attendance division about DeShawn skipping school, he contacted the counselor and principal and described DeShawn's mental state. He asked that they take immediate action. The principal told him that he had suspended the main perpetrators and that a city police officer had arrested them for DeShawn's assault. Anthony also contacted the district superintendant's office to ensure that everyone would follow through.

Although it took a few sessions of intensive counseling with a private counselor, augmented by meetings with his school counselor, DeShawn was able to enjoy a normal life at school. On the home front, his uncle suggested he take guitar lessons, something DeShawn had always wanted to do.

Because of Anthony's willingness to take immediate action when he saw the danger signs of depression in his nephew, DeShawn was able to recover from his horrific bullying experience. Due to the severity of the problem, he felt that the school needed a push in dealing with it. Therefore, rather than take the time to go through channels, Anthony used his common sense and immediately contacted the district superintendent's office. He believed that serious events call for urgent action, and that's exactly what Anthony did to help his nephew survive a bullying episode that could have ended tragically.

As in DeShawn's case, one of the most helpful things you can do when your child is in distress is get all the necessary parties involved in creating a solution to help solve your child's problem.

This team includes your child, you, and possibly your extended family, the school (teachers, counselors, administrators), and, in some cases, the higher levels of school administration. Of course, the first thing you must do is assess the problem to ascertain if it's serious enough to warrant involving all of these parties.

Your child may be able to handle some minor bullying episodes independently. In other cases, you and your child will try to solve the problem together and may not need the school to intervene. However, once you've determined that the bully has jeopardized your child's mental health, and possibly, physical well-being, waste no time in mobilizing whatever help you need.

Something else to consider when figuring out how bullying affects your child is that depression has no age boundaries. Preschool and elementary school children can suffer from the devastating effects of it as well as preteenagers and older children. Ask yourself if your child is showing signs of depression or hopelessness. If she exhibits any of the symptoms listed in this chapter or acts in a markedly different way from her usual pattern, seek help now.

Be Alert to a Major Personality Change in Your Child

Such was the case with Colleen, a second grader and recent transfer from a private school to an affluent suburban elementary school. Born with a severe facial deformity that numerous complicated surgeries only minimally corrected, she found herself the object of three of her classmates' ridicule. They taunted her with vile names like "elephant girl" and "horror flick." On a recent afternoon at recess, the girls surrounded her and chanted, "Join a freak show."

When she came home from school crying, Jim and Dana, her parents, immediately called the principal and told her what had happened. The principal said she'd interview the offenders the next day, as this was the first she'd heard of the incident.

Colleen told her parents that she hated her new school and never wanted to go back. She also shut herself off from her family and cut up the portrait of her that her parents had displayed above the living room sofa.

Colleen's grandmother, Emily, who had a special relationship with her, called to see what she could do to help, but Colleen shocked her by telling her how much she hated herself. She also confided in her older sister that she wanted to die. Although her sister didn't know if she was serious, she immediately told her parents—just in case.

Jim and Dana knew that all of these events were danger signals, so they contacted the school counselor, who referred them to a child psychologist who specialized in childhood depression.

Meanwhile, her parents, knowing that Colleen needed to distance herself from school until the principal dealt with the bullies, kept her home (with the principal's approval) for three days and called the teacher for her assignments.

When the principal contacted the parents of the girls who had bullied Colleen, two of the girls' parents became defensive and said that Colleen didn't belong in a public school because "normal" kids are not prepared to deal with someone who looks so different from the other children.

The remaining girl's parents assured the principal that they would work with their daughter to convince her that bullying Colleen was an unkind act and promised that they would not tolerate any further name-calling or nasty treatment of her classmate. Her parents would also give her the consequence of not allowing her to watch her favorite TV shows after school or to play with her friends on the weekend.

When the principal informed Colleen's parents of the bullies' parents' reactions, they asked to talk to the parents who said their daughter did not belong in that school. The principal agreed, but only if they could all meet with the counselor present.

Although Colleen's parents felt angry and upset about the parents' statements about their daughter, they agreed to meet with them in hopes of educating them about the importance of fair treatment for their daughter and other children who were different in any way.

The counselor moderated the discussion between the parents, and the parents of the girls who bullied Colleen realized the necessity for Colleen to have as normal a life as possible. That included going to school and being treated like all the other children in class. Colleen's parents stressed the point that Colleen didn't expect *special* treatment, but *respectful* treatment. They asked only that their children treat her like any other child in the class.

Once the parents talked to Jim and Dana, they apologized for their insensitive words about Colleen and said that they would talk to their children about how their actions affected Colleen, and that they too would give them consequences for how they had treated Colleen, including having them write letters of apology to Colleen.

The principal also made it clear to all of the parents that if any of the children bothered Colleen again, she would mete out more serious consequences.

Because Jim and Dana recognized the seriousness of their daughter's bullying, they didn't hesitate to get the principal and counselor involved. Had the principal not acted quickly, they would have also contacted the next administrative level because they knew from using their common sense that this was not their daughter's usual behavioral pattern.

Their daughter had been teased about her appearance before but never with this degree of viciousness. Also, their daughter had not previously evidenced signs of sadness that lasted more than a day.

When her parents heard that Colleen had told her sister she wanted to die and when they saw her torn picture, they knew it was time to take serious action. Although they expressed reluctance to talk to the parents of the bullies who did not think their children did anything wrong, they realized that they needed to do that if they were to have some kind of closure and put a stop to the bullying.

Monitor a Persistently Troubling Bullying Situation

Something else you'll want to remember if your child is in distress is the importance of being vigilant in monitoring a persistently troubling bullying situation. Let's say that all signs point to your child being extremely distraught and that he's not functioning the way he usually does, showing a behavior pattern that you're not used to seeing.

All of a sudden, your child's life appears to be back to normal. But is it really? You have to ask yourself if he may be hiding something from you because he's fearful of payback by the bully. Or maybe he's given up, and his depressed state is worsening.

Rather than take for granted that the bullying has come to an abrupt stop, be sure to keep in close touch with your child and the school about what is happening at school, during recess, at lunch, and on the bus.

Sometimes, due to the number of students they're dealing with, it's difficult for school personnel to determine how the bullying is playing out and how your child is dealing with it. On the other hand, your child is in school longer than she's at home, so the school staff may have a better opportunity to monitor the situation.

If you've noticed that your child has stopped communicating about the severe bullying he's experienced or if you notice an abrupt change in behavior on his part (as in the case of the next anecdote, from sadness or depression to a positive mood), then it may be to your advantage to touch base with the teacher, counselor, and principal to learn more about the status of the bullying.

Sometimes, when children suddenly switch their depressed state for one of calmness, it could be a danger signal that the child is suicidal. Although this may not be true in all cases, why take a chance? Keep an eye on your child and watch for any unusual changes in behavior.

Let's observe Brandi, an eighth grader in an all-girl private school, whose life has taken an unhappy turn because of her involvement in a sexting episode. For the past two weeks, Brandi has lived through a grueling episode of cyber bullying at the hands of two girls in the popular crowd.

For six months, Brandi has been dating Austin, a freshman at a local public high school. Recently, he asked Brandi to text him a glamorous picture of herself so he could show her off to his friends. Chloe, the leader of the in-crowd at Brandi's school, dared her to take off her shirt for the picture as a kind of initiation into their group.

At first, Brandi was shocked and recoiled from Chloe's suggestion. But Brandi reluctantly reconsidered because she found it hard to make friends, and her greatest wish was to be part of the popular group.

Chloe and her friends, Ava and Paige, made the photo shoot an event by taking Brandi to Chloe's house while her parents were working. They took turns posing Brandi in a pair of short shorts with a halter top. After she felt comfortable with the outfit, they convinced her that it wouldn't make that much difference if she took off her top.

Her boyfriend would think it was cool, and, of course, it would be for his eyes only. The girls styled her long blonde hair and made her up to look twice her age. In a weak moment, against her better judgment, she agreed to let the girls send the topless pictures to her boyfriend Austin's cell phone.

Because Austin knew that Brandi was not the type of person to walk around without clothes, let alone send this kind of picture out over the Internet, he wondered what would make her do this.

To make matters worse, Chloe and her friends turned on Brandi and forwarded the picture to a number of students in their school. One of the school board members' daughters showed it to her father, who informed the school authorities.

The principal phoned Brandi's parents to make them aware that Brandi could be prosecuted under the state's child pornography laws. Naturally, this turn of events was a complete shock to Tara, Brandi's mother, who did not hear about it until the principal called after hearing from the superintendent's office. Along with Austin, she wondered why her daughter would do something so uncharacteristic.

Subsequently, Tara and her husband, Ben, hired an attorney, who pointed out to the judge that Brandi's so-called friends duped her into the photo shoot. The lawyer was able to save her parents from paying a steep fine, and to save Brandi from an embarrassing blight on her record.

Nevertheless, the whole experience made Brandi sink into a low mood that caused her to withdraw from her parents. She barely ate and spent hours alone in her room crying. To make matters worse, her boyfriend became the butt of his classmates' jokes at his high school.

After Chloe and her friends disseminated the pictures of Brandi, Austin broke up with her because he couldn't deal with the kids at school hounding him to set them up with Brandi, "the hottie."

Brandi's depression deepened to the point where she cut herself off from her family and friends. She attended school but spend most of her days in the dean's office doing her assignments because the girls in her class either shunned her or teased her mercilessly.

Her parents told her that they were taking her to a psychologist who would help her deal with everything that had happened. She tearfully asked them to cancel the appointment because it was useless to talk to anyone. She said she didn't care what happened to her anymore.

Her mother and father were at the point where they were ready to check her into a psychiatric facility because of her mental state, but instead, they said they would keep the appointment and that she didn't have anything to fear. They would accompany her and support her.

However, three days before her appointment, her parents were shocked to see that Brandi appeared to make a complete turnaround in her behavior. She got dressed for school, ate normally, and told her mother that she felt much better and wanted to cancel the appointment with the psychologist. She even offered her younger sister some of her favorite outfits, even though she'd never let her sister borrow any of her clothes before. (Giving away prized possessions is always a danger signal.) She also told her sister that if someone wanted to kill herself pills would be the best way to do it. Of course, her sister told her parents right away.

Tara, her mom, contacted the school that afternoon and spoke to Ms. Morgan, the dean of students, who asked her and her husband, Ben, to come in to talk. What follows is a transcript of that conference.

Tara: As you can imagine, I'm very concerned about Brandi. And today I'm even more troubled by her behavior.

Ms. Morgan: Yes, I've been keeping close watch on her because of what she's been through. I can say that during our talk today she appeared almost like the Brandi I knew before this happened. But I can see from what you said when you called that you agree it's not necessarily a good sign.

Tara: Have the students stopped bothering her, or are things worse?

Ms. Morgan: Mainly, the girls involved are keeping away from her. They've been dealt with and forewarned. If we find anyone harassing her, they're referred to the principal, who will call in their parents and impose consequences, suspending them if necessary.

Tara: Are any of her old friends talking to her?

Ms. Morgan: Yes, the girls who were her friends before this happened are standing by her and are very protective of her. If they even suspect something is amiss, they inform me or the principal.

Tara: I feel that I should keep the appointment with the psychologist. In fact, I've moved it up to tomorrow. Will you keep me informed of any changes you see, or any irregularities in her behavior so that I can stay on top of this?

Ms. Morgan: I'm glad you're taking her to the psychologist sooner. I'll definitely call you if we see any problems. Thanks for coming in.

Tara: We're grateful for your help. I feel better knowing that you're looking out for her and that I know I can call you with any concerns.

When Tara takes Brandi to the psychologist, Dr. Alessi, the doctor tells her that she believes Brandi's depression is serious enough to warrant treatment twice a week. She tells Tara that although Brandi is seriously depressed, she is hopeful about Brandi's prognosis and that Tara did the right thing in keeping the appointment.

On the surface, Brandi appeared to be healing, but inside she was still severely depressed and thinking about suicide. Tara and her husband used their common sense in making the assessment that Brandi's change in behavior and her statements to her sister pointed to a more-impaired mental state rather than a recovery. They knew that she needed professional help and wasted no time in seeking it.

What to Do after the Bullying Stops

What should you do after a bullying episode subsides? Is it wise to put it behind you and your child and forget about it? On the other hand, is it better to stay vigilant and keep an eye on things a while longer?

Your child and you have experienced a strong sense of relief that his mistreatment has stopped and that he can resume living a normal life. However, in most cases, it would help to stay in close contact with the teacher, counselor, and principal and to ask them to keep you informed for a reasonable amount of time after the bullying stops.

You may also want your child to meet with the school counselor periodically to discuss how she's feeling and what she's doing to help herself feel stronger and more confident in the aftermath of her ordeal.

Mainly, you'll want to be your child's lifeline and continue making him feel comfortable telling you when something or someone bothers him. How can you stay on top of how your child is coping on a daily basis? How can you know that he is on the road to recovery after dealing with a bully?

In chapter 9, you'll read more about what you can do to offer your child support so that he grows stronger in spite of his experience with bullying.

KEY POINTS: Chapter 8

- Consider your children's usual behavioral patterns when determining if they are in distress.
- Ask open-ended questions to help your children communicate more effectively.
- Be aware of personality changes in your children.
- If your common sense tells you that something is seriously not right with your children, ask for professional help if you believe you can't handle it on your own.
- When your children are in distress, get all parties involved in creating a solution to help solve the problem.
- Be vigilant in monitoring a persistently troubling bullying problem.
- Stay in close contact with the teacher, counselor, and principal for a reasonable amount of time after the bullying stops. Ask them to keep you informed of any problems.

CHAPTER NINE

~

Be Your Child's Lifeline

Never Keep It Inside

What's the best advice you can give your child about dealing with any type of bully? The number-one thing you can tell your child is that she should never keep serious or persistent acts of bullying to herself. She needs to talk to you when someone is bothering her in a big way.

Telling the teacher and counselor may not be good enough, as they may think your child can handle it himself. Maybe they won't mention it to you because they don't think the incident is serious enough for them to discuss with you. After all, they see kids teasing each other every day and may think that the incident they're witnessing is not cause for alarm.

However, they may not be aware of what happens behind the scenes when no one is watching. In other words, they may not be privy to threats and intimidation or to the escalation of a seemingly harmless bout of teasing.

Keep in mind that if your child believes that another child is teasing her in a lighthearted way or if the teasing is mutual, she may be able to handle it on her own. However, if her instincts tell her that the teasing is hurtful or ongoing, it's time to talk to someone older and wiser, and in most cases, that means you, the parent.

Work at setting a tone in your home that makes your child feel that he can come to you about anything disruptive or troublesome in his life. Then he will feel free to talk to you about what he perceives as a bullying episode, even if he's not sure if it's serious. If your child thinks you believe that he should handle his own problems and not bother you with them, he'll be less likely to open up to you.

Witness a conversation between Tyler, a sixth grader, and Kurt, his father. This is the scene: Tyler is supposed to be doing his math homework, but his father finds him sprawled on the living room couch staring at the wall.

Kurt: Isn't it about time you get started on that math? It's nearly ten o'clock.

Tyler: I'm almost done, Dad. I was taking a little break.

Kurt: Taking a break doesn't get you good grades.

Tyler: I'll get it done. I was just thinking about something I need to work out.

Kurt: Does it have something to do with that kid in your gym class that was calling you names and threatening you? When the gym teacher called your mother, she told him you can take care of yourself. That's what we do in our family, right? We take care of things ourselves.

Tyler: I guess. But sometimes . . .

Kurt: But sometimes what? Are you making excuses? Don't give me any of that. You're a big guy. You can defend yourself. I taught you how.

Tyler: Sometimes it's not that simple. Other kids are getting involved now.

Kurt: sighs and shakes his head. Yes, it is that simple. Just tell those kids you aren't going to take it, and if they keep it up, you'll punch them out.

Tyler: I don't think that will work. You haven't seen these kids.

Kurt: Once they know you mean business, they'll quit. I told you how that worked for me when I was your age. Once I showed them I was stronger than they were, they backed off. And the same will happen for you.

Tyler: You don't understand, Dad. I'll have to find a way, but I'm not going to fight them 'cause it won't work.

Kurt: Believe me, you'll change your mind when you find out they're not going to stop.

Tyler: It might help if I could tell you what's going on.

Kurt: voice rising. I already heard, and it's nothing you can't manage. Making fun of you for having zits—what kind of big deal is that? Listen to me, son. You can talk to me or your teachers all you want, but you're the only one who can stop it. Talk means nothing. So get off your butt and start sticking up for yourself.

Tyler: slams his book down. That's what you always say. And it never works.

He packs up his books and heads to his room. Kurt calls after him, but he has already locked his door.

In the next few weeks, one of the boys bullying Tyler harasses him to the point of tripping him when he walks to his seat in class. He and the other boys call him names like "crater face" and "blotchy boy." They tell him he's so ugly he should dig a hole and bury himself.

His teacher again tries calling home, but gets the same response from his father: Tyler needs to handle it himself. If he stands up to them, they'll stop.

The teacher informs the counselor and administration of the seriousness of the situation. The assistant principal suspends the bullies and schedules a parent conference. Meanwhile, Tyler's father calls the school, demanding to know why they didn't stop the bullying from escalating until it got out of control.

The counselor recommends that the parents talk to the school district social worker, who will connect them with outside resources, professionals who will point out to them the benefits of becoming more willing to listen to Tyler's concerns. They will also encourage them to assist Tyler in coming to a sensible solution to deal with any bullying he may face in the future.

Finally realizing that these bullies aren't going away, Tyler's father agrees to hear what she has to say. Once Kurt becomes part of the solution, Tyler begins to feel hopeful that the bullying will end.

Create a Positive Climate to Discuss Bullying Problems

It would help for you and your child to keep on top of and discuss all bullying situations (that you and she think she can't handle alone) every step of the way. Think of ways you can motivate your child to confide in you from the first time a bully enters her life.

You, better than anyone, know what helps your child and you communicate in the best possible way. If you have open communication all along, it will help create a climate that prompts your child to confide in you.

Compare the parent's approach in the following story with the previous one involving Tyler and Kurt. Listen to a discussion between Adam, age eight, and his father, Marv, regarding Jon, age ten, who has been intimidating Adam in the school yard for the past few days. Jon has threatened to beat Adam up if he doesn't give him his handheld video games.

When Adam refuses to go outside to recess, his second-grade teacher, Ms. Marco, asks him what's wrong. After Adam tells her about Jon's actions, Ms. Marco talks to the counselor. The counselor informs the assistant principal, who alerts school security.

Adam has an open relationship with his father and stepmother Myra and trusted his instincts that told him to tell his teacher about how frightened he felt when Jon confronted him. However, fearing payback from Jon, he asked his father to tell the vice principal and the security guard not to let Jon know he'd said anything about the bullying. At this point, he feared for his safety because Jon had told him he would "bust him up" the next time he made a wrong move.

Watch what happens next:

Adam is helping his father clear away the dinner dishes.

Marv: I want you to know that the assistant principal is going to meet with Jon and his parents tomorrow.

Adam: I told you and Myra that this kid will come after me if anyone finds out I told.

Marv: From what you tell me, he's the type of kid who would come after you whether you told or not.

Adam: I don't want to take a chance. He's huge, Dad, and weighs twice as much as I do. I couldn't fight him off.

Marv: We're not going to let anything happen to you, son. This boy is going to get in trouble for what he did. And the assistant principal promised me that school staff would not make it seem like you told.

Adam: This kid won't believe that. He knows I'm afraid.

Marv: Trust me on this. It will be okay. You did the right thing in telling.

Adam: Maybe you're right, Dad. Now that I think about it, things might change once somebody knows what he's doing. He's been bothering my friend Jacob too.

The next day the principal, assistant principal, and security met with Jon and his parents. The principal suspended Jon for two days. The security officer told him that if he ever threatened Adam again, he would face transfer to another school in the district. Sobered by that fact and by his parents' anger at his actions, Jon never bothered Adam or other students again.

In this instance, Adam trusted his instincts and told his teachers and parents about Jon's mistreatment of him. Even though he initially had misgivings about telling, he came to believe it was the right thing to do and used common sense in acting on his instincts.

Because his parents had created an atmosphere of trust in which he could feel comfortable telling them anything, he was able to tell them about the bullying. If he hadn't told his teacher or parents, the bullying might have intensified and ended in physical or psychological damage to Adam.

Help Your Child Come Up with Ideas

How can you help your child confide in you when something deeply troubles him? I've addressed the importance of active listening, in which you truly take time out to listen to your child without judging or lecturing. In a previous chapter, I've stressed the importance of listening more and giving your opinions less.

If you truly hear what your child is saying, you'll be more likely to get helpful ideas about how to advise her because you'll understand exactly whom she's dealing with and the kind of situation she's up against.

Once you think she's in a receptive mood, you can interject helpful tips that she may want to use when dealing with a bully. You may want to initiate such a conversation using some of these phrases: "How would you feel about trying this?" "Do you think doing x would help?"; or "How did your friend handle it when those kids bothered her?"

Then let your child give his ideas about what steps he'd take to end the bullying. However, if you believe he's thinking of taking an unwise course of action, one that will prolong or intensify the bullying, you'll want to say so.

You could voice your uncertainty about what he's proposing by prefacing your words with these or similar words: "What are some other things you could do? I'm thinking that ignoring him hasn't helped so far"; or, "Let's put our heads together and try to come up with something that will put an end to this."

Suppose your child is not the type who opens up when something bothers her, no matter how hard you've tried to create a rapport, a feeling that she can talk to you about anything without feeling threatened or embarrassed.

If you suspect your child is being bullied and isn't talking about it to you, you can ask another family member, such as a sibling, aunt, uncle, or grandparent with whom she has a strong connection, to convince her to open up about what's going on.

Ask this contact person to try to convince your child to confide in you rather than your asking the contact directly what she said. On the other hand, if the person feels that by not telling you, your child's emotional or physical well-being would be compromised, encourage the person to tell you what your child said. This will give you a starting point for initiating a conversation with your child about the bullying.

Follow Your Instincts about Suspected Bullying

If you think your child is experiencing bullying at school, contact his teacher and counselor. Ask if they've noticed him having problems with other children. If they have, ask them to contact you so that you can work with your child to find a solution. Even if you're not sure, but your instincts tell you that something is happening at school, it's better to ask than to say nothing.

Similarly, if you notice a change in your child's attitude toward school or a disturbing change in behavior, ask the teacher to spend some time observing how your child interacts with classmates. Ask the teacher to keep this confidential so that it will not further aggravate the problem if your child thinks the teacher is watching him. If the teacher notices any problems, ask her to tell you immediately. Sometimes changes in children's behavior are subtle, and the teacher may not notice unless you let her know you're concerned about the possibility your child is unhappy because of something happening at school.

Here's an example of how a grandmother, who is her grandchild's legal guardian, helped with a bullying problem by using her instincts about contacting the school.

A year ago, Juana, a fourth grader, moved from a large Florida city, where everyone spoke Spanish, to a small school district in the same state where there were few Hispanic children or, for that matter, many children from diverse ethnic groups.

Luisa could sense that something was not right with her granddaughter for the past week. For one thing, before Juana caught the bus every morning, she complained of a stomachache and said she wanted to stay home. She also rebuffed the affections of Bonita, her pet calico cat, who was her constant companion since she'd come to live with her grandmother.

Things are not good, Luisa thought. But no matter how gently she tried to broach the subject, Juana would not tell her what was wrong. Luisa had always felt Juana could talk freely to her, but for some reason, she was not able to confide in her about what was now causing her distress.

Her grandmother figured that her current emotional state was school-related because of her reluctance to go to school and the way she moped around the house when she returned home in the afternoon.

She knew that Juana had made a couple of good friends and had invited them to her house on a few occasions. Missy, her closest friend, was helping her learn English, which was a good thing as the school offered a very limited ESL (English as a Second Language) program.

Although Luisa was fluent in English and held down a job as an ER nurse in the local hospital, she felt that Juana would better learn the finer points of English with a peer, especially since her work schedule afforded her limited time.

Luisa decided to take action rather than wait. She knew that Juana was in distress because she didn't seem to find joy in the things that used to excite her, such as reading mystery books (her reading skills were skyrocketing due to help from her friend); baking cookies with her grandmother; or riding her new bike around the neighborhood.

The next day Luisa showed up for an appointment she'd made with Mr. Davis, Juana's teacher. Unbeknownst to Juana, they met in her classroom after school.

Luisa: shaking hands with Mr. Davis. Thanks for seeing me on such short notice, Mr. Davis.

Mr. Davis: Actually, I was going to call you, Ms. Rivera, because of some things that happened. First of all, I've noticed a change in Juana in the past few days. She's progressing well with her English skills, but she doesn't participate in class like she used to.

Luisa: Have you noticed her having any trouble with other kids?

Mr. Davis: I haven't seen anything suspicious in my class, but I'll see if I can find out anything from other staff members and let you know.

Luisa: Thanks for doing that, Mr. Davis. Call me anytime. Here are my work and home numbers.

That next Monday, Luisa answered the phone at work. Mr. Davis called and said that after his conversation with her, he talked to Juana's other teacher and to the lunchroom monitor. He noted that the cafeteria and school yard were prime places for bullying.

Here's a replay of Luisa's conversation with Mr. Davis:

Mr. Davis: The lunchroom monitor told me that two boys from the fifth grade have been bothering Luisa for about a week. They've been making fun of her clothes and saying she's an "illegal immigrant."

Luisa: I suspected something was wrong. She started acting upset and not wanting to go to school about a week ago. Did the lunchroom monitor report it to the principal?

Mr. Davis: I have to be truthful—she hasn't yet. She's been trying to stop it on her own because she says that a lot of kids tease one another.

Luisa: I am very upset about this. It should have been reported right away. Those are hurtful insults we're dealing with here. And if the lunchroom monitor couldn't stop it right away, she should have reported it.

Mr. Davis: I agree. I'm glad you came in the other day, or we wouldn't have known about this. I plan to see the principal first thing tomorrow to report the incident.

Luisa: I'll talk to Juana tonight and try to find out more. I'll be in touch tomorrow before you talk to the principal.

That night after school, Luisa tells Juana that she knows about the boys bothering her. Luisa says she didn't tell her because she didn't want to worry her and because she was afraid of the boys. Luisa tells her that she needs to tell her if anyone bothers her again. When Luisa asks what else the boys did, Juana breaks down in tears.

"They circled me at recess and kept calling me 'Juana from Tijuana' and laughing. One of them even spat on me. They said I'm a foreigner, that I dress and talk like I'm not from this country, and that I should go back to where I came from."

Luisa reaches over and hugs her granddaughter. "You know that's not true. Those are just mean kids talking; so don't listen to anything they say. And spitting is a horrible thing to do to a person."

"I hope they don't try to get even with me because you talked to Mr. Davis," Juana says.

Luisa takes her hand and looks in her eyes. "I don't think you have to worry about those boys anymore. The principal is calling them in, and Mr. Davis will tell me if they ever bother you again."

"The next time I'll tell you sooner if anything happens. I feel better now that you know," Juana says.

"Did anyone try to help you when it happened?"

"My friend Missy and her friends shouted at the boys to go away. They also told the lunch monitor they were bothering me."

Luisa smiles. "It pays to have good friends. Always stay around them and you can help protect one another."

"Okay, abuela. I will do that. And thanks. I think I'll go for a bike ride now!"

The next morning Luisa calls Mr. Davis and fills him in on other things the boys did. After Mr. Davis tells the principal Juana's account of what happened, he suspends the boys and calls their parents for a conference.

Later, he assures Luisa that it will never happen again. He also mentions that he will reprimand the lunchroom monitor about not reporting bullying instances immediately. Had she done this, the problem might not have mushroomed.

Luisa helped her granddaughter by tuning in to signs that told her something was wrong. Since her granddaughter did not follow her usual pattern of confiding in her, she contacted Mr. Davis, Juana's teacher.

She also talked to Juana, who eventually told her about the boys' actions. She made it clear that Juana should stay near friends, enlisting their aid and being willing to help should anyone bully them.

Make Use of the Best Research to Help Your Child

Are you up on the latest research on bullying? Reading books on the topic, accessing the Web, and watching TV programs featuring experts in the field will help you learn the latest and best things to do when a bully pursues your child. But how will you know if you can trust these sources? How will you know if they're reliable?

You can find some of the many authoritative sources about bullying listed in the bibliography at the end of this book. However, every day new and helpful sources will surface, making you wonder how you can determine if they're ones you can count on.

First, consider books. Take into account the author's credentials, but also look at the writer's practical experience. Did the writer work with children in bullying situations, as a therapist, teacher, or counselor, for example, or was he mainly involved in studying the problem academically?

When you peruse the book, take note of its tone and vocabulary. Is it practically written for a broad population, or is it aimed primarily at scholars and researchers? You may find a research-based book that gives practical examples that will suit your needs. It's up to you to decide how you best process and retain information.

Do you like a user-friendly book that employs a readily understandable vocabulary, or do you prefer a more scholarly treatment of the topic? Does the book offer practical ideas that you can apply to your child's bullying experience?

The Internet is also a goldmine brimming with bully-prevention information. However, exercise caution in embracing a website's information by first considering the source of the advice it offers. The federal and state governments sponsor many anti-bullying sites: you have to decide which among them prove most valuable to your child's unique issues.

Many other organizations and individuals also sponsor anti-bullying websites. How do you know if you can trust them? Check to see if the information on the site is in concert with the government and professionally gener-ated research you've read. Also, see if the information is constantly updated or remains the same over a reasonable time period.

While you're at it, look to see if the individual or agency posts a lot of ads on its site, which may mean that it's primarily a moneymaking venture. Ask yourself what the site's main motivation seems to be: to inform you or to generate money for the sponsor?

In any type of media you consult, consider whether it's one person's opinion or data based on reliable research. Most of the information on the research-based sites will offer similar tried-and-tested ideas. Although differ-ent experts may disagree about approaches to handling bullying problems, you will often see a consensus of opinion on the overall principles of bully prevention.

Can you depend on TV shows to offer good information? Consider the biases of the network and the reporters' ability to offer a broad range of ideas and opinions that are research-based in reporting on different topics without advocating any one approach.

If the reporter is fair, she will offer you all the facts to help you decide your best course of action rather than promoting one point of view.

What is your opinion of a given expert that appears on a show? If you can't relate to this person and your common sense tells you that you'll never fol-low his advice because of what he's proclaimed in the past on this and other topics, trust your judgment.

Here's the bottom line in determining whether you should believe re-search is credible: consider the source; think about whether your child would feel comfortable applying the advice given; and trust your common sense in choosing one book, website, or program over another. You live with your child every day, so who better to decide how to help her?

While you'll strive to do everything you can to help your child overcome bullying problems, you'll also want to bolster his confidence to the point that when he encounters a bully, he'll feel strong enough to deal with the stress and frustration he'll experience during a bullying episode.

How can you help your child develop her talents and abilities, which will go a long way in building up her faith in herself?

What are three simple, yet profound words that can help guide your child to a more fulfilling life no matter what he encounters along the way?

In what ways can you model the two qualities of resilience and assertive-ness that will help your child gain strength?

All of these questions and more form the main message of chapter 10.

KEY POINTS: Chapter 9

- Remind your children never to keep serious or persistent bullying problems inside.
- Work at setting a tone in your home that makes your children feel they can come to you about anything disruptive or troublesome in their lives.
- Give helpful tips your children can use when dealing with bullies once you sense they are in a receptive mood.
- Prompt your children to give ideas about what steps they'd take to seek an end to the bullying.
- Ask another family member to encourage your children to open up about what's happening if you suspect they are being bullied and aren't discussing it with you.
- Contact the teacher or counselor to see if they've noticed any problems your children might be having if you think they may be experiencing bullying at school.
- Reading books about bullying, accessing the Web, and watching TV programs featuring experts will help you learn the latest and best things to do when a bully strikes close to home.
- Consider the source of the information you consult; think about whether your children would feel comfortable applying the advice given; and trust your common sense in choosing one book, website, or program over another. That's the bottom line in determining whether you should view information you access as credible.

CHAPTER TEN

Help Your Child
Come Out a Winner

What Does It Take to be a Winner?

Some people picture a child who's a winner as someone who excels in schoolwork, sports, or who is popular in a peer group. Others envision a winner as one who strives to be the best he can be, given his unique interests and abilities.

Some see a winner as a child who keeps trying to reach a goal and never gives up, no matter how formidable the obstacles. A child who shows empathy and concern for others and reaches out to help them when they need it might also exemplify a winner.

What character traits can enhance a child's quest to become a winner, especially when trying to overcome bullying? There are some who would cite resilience, the ability to bounce back no matter how big the challenge, as an admirable quality. Others would add assertiveness to the mix as a necessary trait to help children show their strength in a strong-yet-nonaggressive way during a bout with bullying.

While being a winner may mean different things to each of us, we can all agree that it's essential to help our children achieve a level of confidence and strength that will help them overcome any problems they face in life, especially in the area of bullying.

Encourage Your Child's Interests

One way to boost your child's confidence is to find out what her interests are and to encourage her to develop them in a way that will bring her satisfaction and a sense of pride in mastering what she wants to accomplish.

What else can you do to help your child experience a sense of faith in his abilities beyond providing him with lessons and attending his recitals, games, and concerts? One thing you can do is offer specific praise when he discovers something new and exciting about an interest or reaches a major goal he's been working to attain.

Instead of saying, "Good job playing in that game," you might want to phrase your encouragement like this: "Your great defensive moves helped your team win." The more on target your praise, the more your child will remember it and gain the motivation to repeat his success.

Here's another example: your daughter shows you her painting of the beach you vacationed at last summer. You could glance at the picture as you run out the door and say, "Nice picture." On the other hand, you could make your comment more personal by saying, "Those bright blues and greens make me feel like I'm looking at the beach. And that orange sunset makes the painting glow."

When you praise specific aspects of something your child does well, you'll encourage her to excel in her hobby and find fulfillment in it. And this can help make her stronger in the face of any problem she may encounter.

Try showing an interest in your child's activities to the point that you spend time discussing them with him. Ask questions. Listen to him talk about his interests and hobbies.

Offer to help with projects in a way that enhances the experience for your child, not to take over so that she feels she can't do it without your help (as sometimes happens when parents help kids with homework and school projects). This will help your child experience independence so that she will gain confidence in her decision-making skills, particularly in the process of defending herself against bullying.

Athena, a third grader who moved here with her family from Greece, faces taunts from a couple of girls in her class because she dresses differently from the way they do, and she speaks English with a strong accent.

After meeting with the school counselor, Stefan, Athena's father, decides that joining Girl Scouts and working on badges will give her a sense of pride in herself and will help her make new friends.

Meanwhile, in an effort to change the behavior of the girls bothering Athena, the counselor continues to work with them. The principal meets with their parents following a suspension reinstatement, and they agree to cooperate in persuading their children to stop the bullying and to deliver consequences if it continues.

Here is a conversation between Athena and her father as he drives her home from Girl Scouts.

Stefan: I see that you are working on some interesting badges.

Athena: Yes, Daddy. One is to write a story about a strong woman I know and to introduce her to the class, and the other is to do research about an exciting new hobby.

Stefan: What strong woman will you write about?

Athena: Mom, of course. She put herself through college and became a teacher of nurses at the college. I think that's pretty strong, don't you?

Stefan: Good choice! We can find some pictures of her when she was in high school and the university for the collage you're making.

Athena: Thanks, Daddy. And can you teach me something about playing the guitar because that's what I want to learn for my new hobby. I want to be able to play a song for my troop by the end of the year.

Stefan: That's an excellent goal. I'll be glad to teach you what I know, and I also think we can get a guitar for you in the secondhand music store and sign you up for lessons.

Athena: That would be fun, Daddy. Thanks. I'm so glad I joined Scouts. I've made a new friend this week. Her name is Hope, and we get along great. She's teaching me how to draw.

Stefan: Wonderful! Maybe you can invite her to our home soon. I don't want to upset you, but how are things with those two girls at school?

Athena: They haven't bothered me lately. I heard their parents grounded them. One of them even apologized. I still don't want to be friends with them. I don't think I can trust them. Besides, I'm making new friends at Scouts.

Stefan: I am happy for you, Athena. And you will continue to make new friends. You can be sure of that.

Involve Family Members

Another thing you can do to boost your child's confidence is to ask family members (such as siblings or grandparents) to encourage your child in his interest, hobby, or school project and possibly participate in it with him.

This proved helpful in the case of Dylan, an eighth grader and the son and grandson of well-known funeral-home owners in the small town where he attends middle school.

Since he entered middle school, some classmates and students from other grades have razzed him about his family's funeral business. He's had few invitations to parties, and some students shunned him at lunch and in classes.

Dylan's parents and grandfather forged a relationship with his teacher and the counselor to help ease the stress that he's experiencing due to the constant heckling. Colton, his grandfather, came up with the idea of talking to the class about the funeral business on career day.

Dylan agreed that it wouldn't hurt because most of the kids didn't understand a funeral director's duties, and he felt that if they did, they might not tease him to the extent they did. His grandfather pointed out that maybe the students felt uncomfortable thinking about death. Maybe their teasing had more to do with that than with where he lived or what his parents did. If they turned it into a joke, they wouldn't feel threatened.

The counselor said that no one really knew why the students acted that way, but that the school administration was dealing with it by talking to the offending students and their parents. He also agreed that if Colton spoke about the family business on career day, it would help demystify the profession and help the students look upon Dylan as more of an equal and not a pariah in the school.

Colton showed up at the school dressed in a sport coat and a pair of casual slacks, not the black suit and tie the kids expected. He also broke the mold by steering his classic hot-pink Chevy convertible into the school parking lot rather than taking the hearse the students anticipated seeing him drive.

He explained what he and Dylan's father did on a daily basis without getting technical. The students asked so many questions that the principal, pleased with their response, had to extend the assembly so they could ask more questions.

Because of Colton's rapport with the students and his humorous approach to what could be a somber topic, the students gained some understanding of Dylan and the business his family ran.

Perhaps one of the reasons the students related to him better than they may have to Dylan's father was that he was an older man, albeit what they considered a "cool" one in dress and demeanor, and he reminded them of their own grandfathers.

After Colton's presentation, a couple of the kids who had teased Dylan started acting cautiously polite. And one of the girls he'd asked to the school dance, who had refused because she thought her friends would tease her, changed her mind and agreed to go with him.

Sometimes involving extended family members along with the school staff can help avert or downplay a problem with teasing and exclusion. Of course, if the bullying problem proves to be severe or long lasting, you'll need to involve more people, including professionals such as psychologists, to work on solving the problem.

Affirm Your Child's Positive Qualities

Along with encouraging hobbies and interests and getting the family involved, you can boost your child's confidence by showing gratitude for the little things she does, such as responsibly caring for the family pet or pitching in when you need help around the house.

There are many things you can mention, and they don't have to be big ones. For example, if you see your child experiencing a joyful moment with a friend, you could validate the fact that he is enjoying life despite his problems, "It looks as if you and Drew have a great time playing ball together. I can see how much it means to you to have a friend you can depend on, and I'm sure he feels the same way."

Maybe you've observed your child helping a younger brother or sister with a problem. You might say, "I can see that you have a lot of good ideas to help solve Mikey's problem. You know how to find answers when someone needs help. I believe you'll come up with some creative ideas to solve that problem at school with those kids who are bothering you. And remember—I'm here if you need me just like you're here for Mikey."

If your child appears depressed because of the bullying and cuts herself off from you and other family members, try to find something she's doing at home or school that you can encourage or acknowledge to boost her optimism—for example: "Gran said she loved those cookies you baked for her birthday. Maybe you can make her some for the holidays." Or, "When we went to your conference at school, the teacher said you should try out for the basketball team. She said you're one of her top gym students." A few encouraging words can go a long way in helping your child when he's going through stressful times.

Consider Three Powerful Words

For all of the years I taught, I posted what I consider to be three powerful words on the bulletin board in front of my classroom. At the start of each school year,

I told my classes that in addition to learning how to interpret literature like a professor, speak like a stage actor, and write like Ernest Hemingway, we'd talk about what it takes to excel in life, to find a sense of pride and accomplishment in whatever they chose to do long after they graduated.

If I asked them to recite the three powerful words, they'd shout them out in unison like a mantra. When I asked them if they were living the three words every day, they'd scream, "Yes!"

Even after they left school and launched their careers, they remembered the words. *Self-discipline*, *perseverance*, and *productivity* are the three words that can help your children build themselves up so that they believe they can do anything—even overcome bullying.

When I asked a former student who became an elementary teacher what she remembered most about English class, she said, "I never forgot those three words. When I'm feeling overwhelmed in my job, I think about them, and they help me remember why I teach and how important it is to excel at what I do."

Rich, a mischievous student who surprised everyone by becoming a police officer, said, "If I didn't say those words to myself every day, I'd feel like something was missing, like I'd forgotten to do something I needed to do. Sometimes being out in the patrol car can get rough, and I get discouraged, but those words bring me back to why I'm here in the first place."

The momentum behind these words can offer your children a road map for gaining strength in the face of bullying problems or just about any adversity they face in their lives. Here's why: self-discipline is the key to getting whatever your child sets out to realize in life, be it school success, career achievement, or mastery of an avocation, such as writing, art, sports, or music.

Once your child is able to discipline herself to set a goal, work toward it, and ultimately reach it, she'll gain the momentum to move ahead and realize that goal.

Perseverance means that your child makes a commitment to himself to keep going to attain his goal, to keep running toward the finish line until he blasts through the tape at the end. Sometimes he may feel that he can't go on, that his endurance will not last, but if he perseveres, he'll push himself to keep going until he accomplishes his objective.

It's not an easy order, especially for someone who is trying to extricate herself from a bullying episode. But once your child makes the commitment to persevere, to work with you, the school team, and other supporters until she sees an end in sight, she's won half the battle. Victory is now in clear view and not an elusive dream that will never come to pass.

Help Your Child Build Confidence through Productivity

What implications does the word *productivity* have for a person experiencing bullying? It means your child needs to do his best every day to move forward with something that's meaningful to him, be it nourishing a friendship, reaching an academic goal, or learning more about a hobby or interest.

No matter how your child feels because of what's going on in her life, she needs to do something each day to feel a sense of progress toward a goal. Stress to your child that progress comes mainly from doing something to make the goal materialize. Your child has to take the initiative to produce, to make the goal a reality.

In addition to giving your child a sense of accomplishment, acting productively each day helps cushion the blows that come from dealing with a bully on a daily basis. It gives your child a sense of strength and confidence to know that she's looking forward to something as she works to attain her goal.

You may want to try having your child keep a goal chart. He writes his goal (academic, social, interest, or hobby) at the top of a chart, and briefly outlines what he does each day to move closer to it. Your child will then have a visible record of his progress, and it will motivate him to work harder to reach the goal.

When your child realizes the goal, she'll write a sentence or two telling how working toward it every day helped her get to where she wanted to be. She'll keep the chart as a reminder that by being productive and doing something each day to realize her dream, she'll usually accomplish that goal. After reaching her goal, she can begin a new chart with a new goal.

Becoming engaged in a task, actually becoming so involved in what you're doing that you get totally lost in it in a pleasant way so that the work you're doing eclipses the problems in your life, is one of the benefits and by-products of productivity. It's a paradox, but when your child loses himself in a task and he's totally caught up in it, he'll be better able to find himself.

Here's an example of how engagement in a task changed things for Summer, a seventh-grade student in an inner-city middle school. Her parents could not care for her due to mental-health issues and economic problems, and she now resides in St. Vincent's Group Home. Her social worker, Carlos (he goes by his first name since he's not that much older than his charges), became concerned when Summer's counselor asked him to come in to discuss a bullying episode involving Summer.

As it turned out, a group of girls from another school roughed her up at the public bus stop. They had set out to steal the stylish jacket her grandmother had recently sent her for her birthday, and Summer resisted. Luckily, the police appeared on the scene in a flash.

The girls were charged with attempted robbery and assault, and a hearing date was set. Before the incident, the same girls had been harassing Summer by calling her "orphan girl" and saying things like, "Look at you. No wonder your parents don't want you"; and "Why were you ever born?"

Due to the psychological and physical assaults, Summer suffered from nightmares and refused to go to the bus stop. Carlos took her to the doctor, who prescribed a mild tranquilizer to be taken temporarily. He also started dropping her off at school each morning. At the same time, Summer met regularly with the counselor with Carlos in attendance.

At one of these conferences, Carlos suggested an idea that had helped with one of his students who faced a similar situation. He put out the idea of helping Summer work toward a goal of accomplishing something she had shown a strong interest in to help bolster her self-confidence and to take her mind off the anxiety that had dominated her life since the bullying started.

Carlos thought about how Summer helped him put together the St. Vincent Home's newsletter and how she'd lost herself in the task while her housemates were watching TV or playing ball in the yard. He wondered if writing for the school newspaper might help Summer get out of the rut she was in.

Her English teacher, thinking along the same lines, had mentioned to the counselor that there was an opening for a features writer on the paper, and she thought that given Summer's creative writing savvy, she'd be a shoo-in for the job.

When Carlos asked Summer if she'd be interested in applying for the feature writing position at school, it was the first time since the bullying began that she'd shown interest in anything outside of reading novels alone in her room.

The next day, Summer applied for the job. The job spec that the teacher posted on the school bulletin board asked for a features writer who would not be afraid to speak out on an issue. Summer assured the teacher/sponsor that she was ready to do just that.

Fortunately, she got the job over three other students who applied. Her first assignment was to write an article about the school's need for English classes for students from other countries. As it stood, there was little funding allocated for English as a Second Language classes, and these students were left to fend for themselves.

When Carlos asked Summer how her article was progressing, she showed him the rough draft, which surprised and amazed him for its insights and writing skill. He also observed that she was beginning to socialize with her housemates and had stopped spending so much time alone in her room.

As a result of Summer's article and the discussions it set off in the community, the school board drafted a resolution to increase instruction for students who found themselves struggling to learn a new language.

When Summer saw the impact her article had on her classmates and the community, she began thinking about writing an article about bullying. She wanted to help other students avoid the pain that she had suffered at the hands of her tormenters.

Eventually, she wrote an article that brought to light her and other students' experiences with bullying. She wrote it in the form of an open letter to her school entitled: "Don't Let the Bullies Get You Down: An Open Letter from Someone Who's Been There."

The article caused such a stir in the community (the local newspaper picked it up and reprinted it on their op-ed page) that the school administration decided to incorporate a bullying education program into the curriculum.

The program would reach across different subject areas and would give kids practical tips about how to protect themselves against bullies, how to deal with bullies, and how to take care of themselves while the bullying was playing out.

The following year, the teacher made Summer the new features editor. Because of her total engagement in the task of writing for the paper, Summer began to garner new confidence that transferred to her social life at school.

She made new friends among her fellow writers and looked forward, as she never had before, to attending school each day. She told Carlos that he no longer had to drive her to school; she'd rather take the bus with a friend because she was no longer afraid.

The girls who bullied her were sentenced in juvenile court for assault and never returned to the middle school again.

Carlos was a dedicated mentor to Summer, and he knew that being productive by writing for the school paper would help her move forward from the traumatic events she'd experienced at the hands of bullies. He believed that once she became engaged in the task of writing, she'd be on the road to recovery and living a happy life.

In this case, the object of Summer's engagement was writing for the paper. In other cases, it may be volunteerism, mastery of a school subject, drama, sports, or any number of other hobbies or unique interests your child may possess.

The important thing is that he becomes engaged in a task that will afford him some relief from the stresses that bullying brings and will, at the same time, boost his confidence. Being productive in achieving that goal will help him move forward in his life.

Model Two Winning Behaviors

Modeling helpful qualities, namely resilience and assertiveness, will influence your child more than will most other ways of helping her bear up under the strain of bullying. If you give her advice, she may listen, but if you *show* her how to implement these positive behaviors by modeling them, she will be more likely to try them.

Why is resilience a helpful quality to have while dealing with a bully? It means that no matter what happens in your life, you're able to lift yourself up and keep moving ahead. Of course, your child may feel sad, upset, or angry, or a combination of these emotions when a bully confronts him. But showing resilience means he will, in time, be able to rise above these emotions and keep moving toward a solution that will bring some kind of resolution.

How can you, as a parent, model resilience? We have the chance every day to show our children how it's possible to bounce back from the problems, from the small ones to the heavy ones, that life deals us.

Say you apply for a promotion that you really want and for which you are highly qualified. You find out that your employer chooses another person, one she knows socially, even though that person does not have the proper credentials. You can't complain because you don't have a union, and maybe your boss may not look favorably upon you the next time a promotion comes up.

Your child hears you and your husband talking about how the boss skipped over you for a personal friend. You can choose to show your anger about the unfairness of it in front of your child and say you're going to going to quit your job. Or you can choose, instead, to state that you believe you should have gotten the job because you had all the perfect qualifications for it.

You might also say that when you applied for the job, you knew that sometimes bosses choose people for reasons other than their qualifications. Maybe the boss knew something about the other candidate that you didn't, and that's why she chose him. Or maybe the selection process was totally unfair, but you knew that to complain too loudly might hurt your chances for another promotion.

We know we won't always get what we deserve, but we have the option of voicing our disappointment to the person in charge and doing the best we can to have him reconsider. However, if our best efforts don't work, we can show resilience and not let the event dominate our lives.

Suppose a more traumatic event happens. A neighbor who is jealous begins to spread false stories about you behind your back. Your child has heard you and your sister talking about how to handle this problem, and she knows that you're concerned about what will happen.

You can show your child how you can deal with this kind of problem by saying, "I know you overheard Aunt Kelly and me talking on the phone about the things Ms. Cramer is saying. I know that what she said isn't true and that upsets me a lot, but I'm not going to let it affect the way I live my life. I have my friends, and I trust they won't believe what she's saying because they are my friends. I'm angry and disappointed that she's doing this, but I'm trying my best not to pay attention to it."

It's not enough to say it to your child, but you'll want to reinforce your message about how what you're going through is only one part of your life, not all of it. In this case, let your child see you going about your day without giving what your neighbor did too much of your time or attention.

Of course, it's healthy to acknowledge it, to express your feelings about it, and to do what you can to rectify it, but it's not healthy to dwell on it and give it power. If this is how you'd want your child to react to a similar situation in her life, model it for her.

Just as showing resilience in the face of troublesome events in life can help make living in the worst of circumstances (in your child's case, bullying) more bearable, learning to act assertively in tackling a bullying problem can be a valuable skill. Your child can be assertive in a variety of ways. And that doesn't mean going after the bully physically, because that can cause the bully to come back at him.

Rather, it means assuming an aura of strength and confidence and being willing to say something to the bully if your child's common sense tells her that it's wise to do so. It also means having the courage to tell you or a school staff member if she feels it's unwise to take the matter into her own hands by speaking to the bully.

How can you model assertiveness for your child? A simple encounter with an aggressive salesperson trying to sell you something you don't want presents a good scenario for showing how assertive behavior can get someone you don't want to converse with to stop bothering you.

Let's listen in on a conversation between Grace (mother of Trey, age nine) and a telephone solicitor who calls just as the family is about to sit down for dinner.

Trey, his younger sister, and Dad are already seated, waiting for Grace to hang up the phone so that they can start eating.

Phone Lady: Ms. Aims, I wanted to tell you about our special offer on gold jewelry for the holidays.

Grace: We're about to sit down to eat, so this is a bad time.

Phone Lady: Have you ever ordered jewelry online before? The discounts are amazing.

Grace: I'm sure they are, but I need to hang up now.

Phone Lady: I understand, but I'd like to call at a later date. You don't want to miss out on these bargains. And they're only available for a limited time.

Grace: No, don't call again, especially since I'm on the "do not call" list.

Phone Lady: Sorry to bother you. Thanks for your time.

Grace hangs up.

Grace makes the phone call as short as possible and speaks assertively so as not to prolong the conversation. Trey, who is starting to shovel spaghetti in his mouth, asks his mother why she didn't hang up instead of talking to the lady.

"Some people may want to do that, but I felt more comfortable doing what I did. I was able to get my point across that I didn't want to buy her jewelry. And I don't think she'll be calling back."

"I'm sure she won't," Trey said. "I guess you told her."

There are many other occasions that call for modeling assertive behavior, for example, someone pushes you to chair a Cub Scout committee, and you are already overbooked; a neighbor insists you try a rich dessert she brings over when you've just started a diet; or your friend continues talking nonstop to you on the phone when all you want is a few minutes to yourself.

You can also show assertive behavior when dealing with your own children every day. You can model this behavior by telling your children exactly what you expect of them. State what you want them to do in as few words as possible.

Try not to show extreme anger or emotion if they don't meet your expectations, but emphasize what more they need to do in a businesslike, calm tone. State the consequences you'll deliver if they don't do what you requested. Don't engage in arguments. State what you want them to do; then expect them to follow through.

If they don't do what you want them to do or disregard a rule, give the consequences you promised. If you deal with your children assertively rather than aggressively when you want them to do something or when breaking a firmly established rule, you'll help them by presenting them with a model for assertiveness that they can carry with them throughout their lives in the home, in school, and in the workplace.

You'll find many opportunities to model assertive behavior and to show your child that being assertive in tense or awkward situations can build confidence and make him feel that he's in charge and more in control of a situation. And that goes a long way when your child is dealing with bullies, who can deflate his confidence and sense of control over his life.

Help Your Child Look to the Future with a Winning Attitude

Throughout this book, I've stressed the importance of using common sense in dealing with bullies. Encourage your children to use common sense and logic in addressing teasing, ignoring, intimidation, physical abuse, and any type of bullying they encounter.

I've also emphasized that your child cannot overcome a bullying problem alone. Of course, if the problem is minor and short-lived he can try to handle it himself first. However, for more pressing bullying issues, he'll need your help. Sometimes, he'll want you to listen and empathize, and possibly give input, while other times he'll need you to assume a more active role.

Sometimes your child will need the school's help to monitor and actively intervene when necessary. Therefore, it's prudent to maintain a close and cooperative relationship with school personnel in order to accomplish the things you want done.

Your child's extended family can offer support by listening to her concerns and by lifting her spirits when she needs a boost. Moreover, she needs everyone, including herself, to work together to find a resolution to the problems she's facing.

If everyone is aware of what is happening and is rooting for her, she can't help but come out on top. If one person on the team is not fully informed about what is going on, the other can jump in and help deal with problems as they crop up. One person alone cannot handle a major bullying problem that can cause heartache, depression, and worse.

You'll also want to impress upon your child that things will change, that there will be a day when he won't be in the position of having to worry that someone will harass or intimidate him. The bullying will leave his life as surely as it invaded it. If he recognizes that bullying is not forever, that it will end, he will be free to look forward to a life without fear, anxiety, or sadness.

While most people aspire to live life in the present, they also desire to look ahead. Looking forward to a future without bullying will help sustain your child and lift her up even when it doesn't seem like things will be as they once were.

You are the most important person to help your children find that peace and optimism, a peace they will realize when the bullying stops.

KEY POINTS: Chapter 10

- Help your children achieve a level of confidence and strength that will aid them in overcoming any problems they may face.
- Learn about your children's interests, and encourage their development.
- Give your children specific praise when they work toward a major goal.
- Offer to help your children with their projects in a way that enhances the experience. Let them lead the way.
- Enlist family members to encourage your children in an interest, a hobby, or a school project.
- Show gratitude for the things your children do to help you.
- Stress three powerful words: *self-discipline*, *perseverance*, and *productivity* to jump-start your children's confidence.
- Encourage your children to become engaged in a task to afford them relief from the stress bullying brings and to boost confidence.
- Model resilience and assertiveness to help your children gain strength.
- Help your children sustain a positive attitude to overcome bullying.

~

Selected Bibliography

Books for Parents and Teachers

Alexander, Jenny. *When Your Child Is Bullied: An Essential Guide for Parents*. London: Simon and Schuster, 2007.

Helps parents know which steps to take to encourage their children's self-confidence to protect them from bullies.

Carpenter, Deborah, and Christopher J. Ferguson. *The Everything Parent's Guide to Dealing with Bullies: From Playground Teasing to Cyber Bullying, All You Need to Ensure Your Child's Safety and Happiness*. Avon, MA: Adams Media, 2009.

Everything you want to know about bullies, victims, and bystanders, plus tips for bully-proofing your child.

Coloroso, Barbara. *The Bully, the Bullied, and the Bystander: From Preschool to High School—How Parents and Teachers Can Help Break the Cycle*. New York: Harper Resource, 2009.

Author explains the roles of each of the participants in bullying mentioned in the title and suggests ways to change their behaviors for the better.

DePino, Catherine. *Real Life Bully Prevention for Real Kids: 50 Ways to Help Elementary and Middle School Students*. Lanham, MD: Rowman and Littlefield, 2009.

Kid-friendly classroom activities to help children beat the bullying cycle.

Horne, Dr. Arthur M., Dr. Jennifer L. Stoddard, and Christopher D. Bell, *A Parents' Guide to Understanding and Responding to Bullying: The Bully Buster's Approach*. Champaign, IL: Research Press, 2008.

Helps parents and teachers build skills that will help children cope with bullying.

McMullen, Carol S. *The Bully Solution: A Parent's Guide: Effective and Practical Ways to Empower Your Child and Stop Bullying in Its Tracks*. New York: Scholastic, 2009.
　Helps families solve different types of bullying issues wherever they occur.

Olweus, Dan. *Bullying at School: What We Know and What We Can Do*. Cambridge, MA: Blackwell, 1993.
　Gives parents, teachers, and principals valuable information about how to recognize and deal with bullying.

Rigby, Ken. *Children and Bullying: How Parents and Educators Can Reduce Bullying at School*. Malden, MA: Wiley-Blackwell, 2009.
　Combines research with advice about bullying.

Scaglione, Joanne, and Arrica Rose Scaglione. *Bully-Proofing Children: A Practical, Hands-On Guide to Stop Bullying*. Lanham, MD: Rowman and Littlefield, 2006.
　Gives parents and teachers tips, stories, and scripts to help children deal with bullying.

Willard, Nancy E., and Karen Steiner. *Cyberbullying and Cyberthreats: Responding to the Challenge of Online Social Aggression, Threats, and Distress*. Champaign, IL: Research Press, 2007.
　Gives counselors, administrators, teachers, and parents important information about how to prevent all types of cyber bullying and what to do when it occurs.

Wiseman, Rosalind. *Queen Bees and Wannabees: Helping Your Daughter Survive Cliques, Gossip, Boyfriends, and the New Realities of Girl World*. New York: Three Rivers Press, 2009.
　Discusses how girls interact with one another and its implications for bullying. Gives strategies to help parents raise strong daughters.

Books for Children

Anderson, Mary Elizabeth. *Gracie Gannon: Middle School Zero*. Windsor, CA: Rayve Productions, 2008.
　Ages 9–12. Gives a fictional account of a girl's adjustment to middle school and the problems it brings.

Burton, Bonnie. *Girls against Girls: Why We Are Mean to Each Other and How We Can Change*. San Francisco: Orange Avenue Publishing, 2009.
　Ages 12–16. Author addresses girl bullying from the standpoint of both bullies and victims.

Cosby, Bill. *The Meanest Thing to Say: A Little Book for Beginning Readers*. New York: Scholastic, 1997.
　Ages 4–8. Helps kids deal with bullies while helping them see the goodness in everyone.

Criswell, Patti Kelly, and Angela Martini. *A Smart Girl's Guide to Friendship Troubles*. Middleton, WI: American Girl, 2003.

Ages 9–12. Gives practical advice for girls with friendship problems.

DePino, Catherine. *Blue Cheese Breath and Stinky Feet: How to Deal with Bullies*. Washington, D.C.: Magination Press, 2004.

Ages 4–8. Offers advice in a fictional setting on how a bullied child can use a unique defense plan against bullies.

———. *In Your Face, Pizza Face: A Girl's Bully Busting Book*. Weaverville, CA: Boulden Publishing, 2008.

Ages 9–12. Deals with relational aggression in a fiction format. Relates how a girl uses her ingenuity to foil bullies.

Estes, Eleanor, and Louis Slobodkin. *The Hundred Dresses*. Orlando, FL: Harcourt, 2004.

Ages 9–12. Addresses the painfulness of teasing in an enchanting story.

Green, Susan. *Don't Pick on Me: Help for Kids to Stand Up to and Deal with Bullies*. Oakland, CA: Instant Help Books, 2010.

Ages 9–12. Employs short activities to help kids cope with bullying.

Ludwig, Trudy. *Just Kidding*. Berkeley: Tricycle Press, 2006.

Ages 4–8. Deals with teasing in a fictional framework. Provides conversation prompts for discussion for parents and children.

Ludwig, Trudy, and Beth Adams. *Confessions of a Former Bully*. Berkeley: Tricycle Press, 2010.

Ages 9–12. Tells what's in a bully's head and what victims can do to defend themselves. Fictional musings of a former bully.

Ludwig, Trudy, and Abigail Marble. *My Secret Bully*. NY: Tricycle Press, 2005.

Ages 4–8. Deals with exclusion and isolation and the importance of a bullied child communicating with a parent.

McCain, Becky Ray, and Todd Leonardo. *Nobody Knew What to Do*. Morton Grove, IL: Albert Whitman and Company, 2001.

Ages 4–8. A touching story that emphasizes the power of bystanders in stopping bullying.

McCord, Pat Mauser. *A Bundle of Sticks*. Wethersfield, CT: Turtle Press, 2004.

Ages 4–8. Relates in story form how a boy finds his inner strength in dealing with a bully.

Moore, Julianne, and Le Uyen Pham. *Freckleface Strawberry and the Dodgeball Bully*. New York: Bloomsberry USA Books, 2009.

Ages 4–8. Humor enhances this story about bullies that many kids will relate to and learn from.

Moss, Peggy. *Say Something*. Gardiner, ME: Tilbury House, 2008.
Ages 4–8. Deals with the role of the bystander in bullying.

O'Neill, Alexis, and Laura Huliska Beith. *The Recess Queen*. New York: Scholastic, 2002.
Ages 3–7. School yard bully learns kindness from a new girl in the class.

Romaine, Trevor. *Bullies Are a Pain in the Brain*. Minneapolis, MN: Free Spirit Publishing, 1997.
Ages 9–12. Nonfiction book in cartoon form that offers kids sound advice about dealing with bullies.

Spinelli, Jerry. *Crash*. New York: Laurel Leaf, 2004.
Ages 9–12. Tells the story of a seventh grader's change from a smug kid to a caring young man.

Tolle, Eckhart, Robert S. Friedman, and Frank Riccio. *Milton's Secret*. Charlottesville, VA: Hampton Roads Publishing Company, 2008.
Ages 4–8. Offers the story of a protagonist who learns how to abandon his fear of being bullied. A dose of Tolle's "living in the now" philosophy for children.

Webster-Doyle, Terrence. *Why Is Everybody Always Picking on Me: Guide to Handling Bullies*. Middlebury, VT: Atrium Society, 1999.
Ages 9–12. Teaches kids self-respect and helps them learn to solve problems without turning to violence.

Online Resources

Internet Pages

APA.org. "How Parents, Teachers, and Kids Can Take Action to Prevent Bullying." Accessed January 10, 2010. http://www.apa.org/helpcenter/bullying.
Gives helpful and psychologically sound advice about bully prevention. Lists additional resources.

KidsHealth. "Helping Kids Deal with Bullies." Accessed January 10, 2010. http://www.Kidshealth.org.
Click on parents', kids', or teens' site. Then type "dealing with bullies" in the search line to see this and other articles like it. The site helps kids deal with specific information about bullying. Includes helpful tips for younger children and teens. Audio helps reinforce the messages.

Public Broadcasting System. "It's My Life." Accessed January 10, 2010. http://www.PbsKids.org/itsmylife/.
Offers entertaining and useful tips and videos about school and family life, and an interesting selection of videos about bullying.

Selected Websites Dealing with Bullying

http://www.adl.org/bibliography.

The anti-defamation league of B'nai B'rith sponsors this helpful website. Click on "prejudice and discrimination." Then click on "bullying and name-calling" for a comprehensive reading list for kids about bullying.

http://www.olweus.org.

Touted as the world's foremost bully prevention program, this site offers tips for parents and school personnel. It also offers useful pointers on how to talk with educators about bullying.

http://www.opheliaproject.org.

Deals with relational aggression and gives excellent information about bullying among girls. Resources abound for youth, parents, and teachers.

http://www.stopbullyingnow.hrsa.gov/ADULTS.

U.S. Department of Health and Human Services (Health Resources and Services Administration).

Click on "What Kids Can Do" and "What Adults Can Do." Offers statistics and useful tips for parents and kids. Kids' section includes interesting games and videos.

About the Author

Dr. Catherine DePino has written numerous books for children and teachers, including two chapter books, *Blue Cheese Breath and Stinky Feet: How to Deal with Bullies* and *In Your Face, Pizza Face*, and a resource book for teachers, *Real Life Bully Prevention for Real Kids*. She has also written books, such as *Grammar Workout*, about writing improvement.

The author holds a doctorate in curriculum theory and development and educational administration, a master's in English education, and a bachelor's in English and Spanish education from Temple University.

She served as an English teacher, department head, and disciplinarian in the Philadelphia School District. During her years as an educator, she dealt with and remediated bullying on a daily basis. She served as a teacher of high school English and adult education and taught all grade and ability levels from remedial to gifted.

As a student teaching supervisor at Temple University, the author emphasized the importance of helping students become lifelong learners by giving them the tools to teach themselves.

Her special interests lie in the areas of bully prevention, alternative assessment, cooperative learning, and proactive discipline. Access her website at www.catherinedepino.com.